Q: Skills for Success
READING AND WRITING

2

Joe McVeigh

Jennifer Bixby

SERIES CONSULTANTS

Marguerite Ann Snow

Lawrence J. Zwier

VOCABULARY CONSULTANT

Cheryl Boyd Zimmerman

OXFORD

UNIVERSITY PRESS

OXFORD
UNIVERSITY PRESS

198 Madison Avenue
New York, NY 10016 USA

Great Clarendon Street, Oxford OX2 6DP UK

Oxford University Press is a department of the University of Oxford.
It furthers the University's objective of excellence in research, scholarship,
and education by publishing worldwide in

Oxford New York

Auckland Cape Town Dar es Salaam Hong Kong Karachi
Kuala Lumpur Madrid Melbourne Mexico City Nairobi
New Delhi Shanghai Taipei Toronto

With offices in

Argentina Austria Brazil Chile Czech Republic France Greece
Guatemala Hungary Italy Japan Poland Portugal Singapore
South Korea Switzerland Thailand Turkey Ukraine Vietnam

OXFORD and OXFORD ENGLISH are registered trademarks of
Oxford University Press in certain countries.

© Oxford University Press 2011

Database right Oxford University Press (maker)

General Manager, American ELT: Laura Pearson
Publisher: Stephanie Karras
Associate Publishing Manager: Sharon Sargent
Managing Editors: Martin Coleman, Mary Whittemore
Associate Development Editors: Rebecca Mostov, Keyana Shaw
Director, ADP: Susan Sanguily
Executive Design Manager: Maj-Britt Hagsted
Associate Design Manager: Michael Steinhofer
Electronic Production Manager: Julie Armstrong
Production Artist: Elissa Santos
Cover Design: Molly Scanlon
Image Manager: Trisha Masterson
Image Editors: Robin Fadool and Liaht Pashayan
Production Coordinator: Elizabeth Matsumoto

ISBN: 978-0-19-475623-5 Reading Writing 2 Student Book Pack
ISBN: 978-0-19-475639-6 Reading Writing 2 Student Book
ISBN: 978-0-19-475621-1 Q Online Practice Student Access Code Card

Printed in China

This book is printed on paper from certified and well-managed sources.

10 9 8 7 6 5 4 3 2 1

ACKNOWLEDGMENTS

*The publisher would like to thank the following for their permission to reproduce
copyrighted material:* p. 31 "The Color of Business" from "What Color Is
Business?" by Orwig Marketing Strategies. Copyright © 2004 Orwig
Marketing Strategies, http://www.orwig.net. Used by permission; p. 112
"I Hate Machines!" from "Self-Service World" by Sheila Moss, http://www.
humorcolumnist.com. Copyright Sheila Moss. Used by permission; p. 132
from "In Praise of the Throwaway Society" by Anthony Forte, http://www.
madanthony.net. Used by permission of the author; p. 146 from "The Hoca
and the Candle" in Watermelons, Walnuts, and the Wisdom of Allah: And
Other Tales of the Hoca by Barbara K. Walker, illustrated by Harold Berson.
Copyright © 1991Texas Tech University Press. Used by permission.

*The publishers would like to thank the following for their kind permission to reproduce
photographs:* Cover Yukmin/Asia Images/Getty Images; Jupiter Images/
Workbook Stock/Getty Images; David Anderson/iStockphoto; 4x6/
iStockphoto; Kuzma/iStockphoto; TrapdoorMedia/iStockphoto; vi Marcin
Krygier/iStockphoto; xii Rüstem GÜRLER/iStockphoto; p. 2 REUTERS/Bob
Strong; p. 4 David J. Green - lifestyle themes/Alamy (facebook); p. 4 Zooid
Pictures (news); p. 6 Bubbles Photolibrary/Alamy; p. 7 Jose Luis Pelaez/Blend
Images/Corbis UK Ltd.; p. 12 Design Pics Inc/Rex Features; p. 22 Fred R.
Conrad/The New York Times/Redux; p. 24 Tina Tyrell/Tina Tyrell Photography
(blue); p. 24 Tina Tyrell/Tina Tyrell Photography (brown); p. 24 Tina Tyrell/
Tina Tyrell Photography (green); p. 24 Masterfile UK Ltd. (red); p. 27 Steve
Vidler/Superstock Ltd.; p. 31 Charles Rex Arbogast/AP Photo/Press Association
Images; p. 35 Masterfile UK Ltd.; p. 42 Emily Keegin/Getty Images; p. 46 Age
Fotostock /Superstock Ltd. (handshake); p. 46 Getty Images (talking);
p. 47 Artiga Photo/Corbis UK Ltd.; p. 62 REUTERS/Will Burgess; p. 67 Mike
Hewitt/FIFA/Getty Images; p. 71 John Wollwerth/Shutterstock (track);
p. 71 Andy Wong/Associated Press/Press Association Images (race);
p. 84 www.jupiterimages.com/Getty Images (birthday); p. 84 Tim Hall/Getty
Images (telephone); p. 84 Inti St Clair/Blend Images/Getty Images (game);
p. 84 Blend Images/Oxford University Press (bedtime); p. 87 Radius Images/
Alamy (place setting); p. 87 House of An/RFPR Inc. (restaurant); p. 88 House of
An/RFPR Inc.; p. 91 Richard Levine/Alamy; p. 92 Jerry Arcieri/Corbis UK Ltd.;
p. 102 terry harris just greece photo library/Alamy; p. 104 Kevin Moloney/
Getty Images (ordering); p. 104 BWAC Images/Alamy (supermarket);
p. 104 Henry George Beeker/Alamy (airport); p. 104 Sipa Press/Rex Features
(photo kiosk); p. 113 Blend Images/Oxford University Press; p. 115 Peter
Arnold, Inc./Alamy (rowing); p. 115 Nick White/Getty Images (line);
p. 117 Blend Images/Alamy; p. 126 Ianni Dimitrov/Alamy; p. 127 Blend
Images/Alamy (cobbler); p. 127 Blend Images/Alamy (recycling);
p. 167 Edward Gibson; p. 173 Northfield Mount Hermon School;
p. 177 Sabine Scheckel/The Image Bank/Getty Images; p. 186 Big Cheese
Photo LLC/Alamy (sneeze); p. 186 Nigel Cattlin /Alamy (mosquito);
p. 186 Janine Wiedel Photolibrary/Alamy (x-ray); p. 186 DPA/Press Association
Images (blood test); p. 186 Neil White/Rex Features (beach); p. 186 Flirt/
Superstock Ltd. (asthma); p. 195 Games Press Ltd.

Illustrations by: p. 4 Claudia Carlson; p. 26 Stanford Kay; p. 44 Stanford Kay;
p. 51 Stanford Kay; p. 52 Stanford Kay; p. 53 Stanford Kay; p. 64 Stuart
Bradford; p. 106 Claudia Carlson; p. 124 Karen Minot; p. 144 Harry Briggs;
p. 146 Jing Jing Tsong; p. 147 Jing Jing Tsong; p. 164 Claudia Carlson;
p. 166 Stuart Bradford; p. 173 Stuart Bradford; p. 174 Claudia Carlson.

ACKNOWLEDGEMENTS

Authors

Joe McVeigh holds a B.A. in English and American Literature from Brown University and an M.A. in TESOL from Biola University. He has taught at Middlebury College, the University of Southern California, the California Institute of Technology, and California State University, Los Angeles. Joe has also lived and worked overseas in the U.K., Hungary, China, India, and Chile. He has presented nationally and internationally on topics including methods and techniques for teaching reading, intercultural communication, and testing and assessment. He works independently as a consultant, teacher-trainer, workshop presenter, author, and editor.

Jennifer Bixby holds an M.A. in TESOL from Boston University. She has taught students of various ages in Colombia, Japan, and the U.S in a wide variety of programs, including community colleges and intensive English programs in the U.S. Her interests lie in the development of high-interest materials and in the teaching of writing.

Series Consultants

Marguerite Ann Snow holds a Ph.D. in Applied Linguistics from UCLA. She is a professor in the Charter College of Education at California State University, Los Angeles where she teaches in the TESOL M.A. program. She has published in *TESOL Quarterly*, *Applied Linguistics*, and *The Modern Language Journal*. She has been a Fulbright scholar in Hong Kong and Cyprus. In 2006, she received the President's Distinguished Professor award at Cal State L.A. In addition to working closely with ESL and mainstream public school teachers in the U.S., she has trained EFL teachers in Algeria, Argentina, Brazil, Egypt, Japan, Morocco, Pakistan, Spain, and Turkey. Her main interests are integrated content and language instruction, English for Academic Purposes, and standards for English teaching and learning.

Lawrence J. Zwier holds an M.A. in TESL from the University of Minnesota. He is currently the Associate Director for Curriculum Development at the English Language Center at Michigan State University in East Lansing. He has taught ESL/EFL in the U.S., Saudi Arabia, Malaysia, Japan, and Singapore. He is a frequent TESOL conference presenter, and has published many ESL/EFL books in the areas of test-preparation, vocabulary, and reading, including *Inside Reading 2* for Oxford University Press.

Vocabulary Consultant

Cheryl Boyd Zimmerman is Associate Professor of TESOL at California State University, Fullerton. She specializes in second-language vocabulary acquisition, an area in which she is widely published. She teaches graduate courses on second-language acquisition, culture, vocabulary, and the fundamentals of TESOL, and is a frequent invited speaker on topics related to vocabulary teaching and learning. She is the author of *Word Knowledge: A Vocabulary Teacher's Handbook*, and Series Director of *Inside Reading*, both published by Oxford University Press.

REVIEWERS

We would like to acknowledge the advice of teachers from all over the world who participated in online reviews, focus groups, and editorial reviews. We relied heavily on teacher input throughout the extensive development process of the Q series, and many of the features in the series came directly from feedback we gathered from teachers in the classroom. We are grateful to all who helped.

UNITED STATES Marcarena Aguilar, North Harris College, TX; **Deborah Anholt**, Lewis and Clark College, OR; **Robert Anzelde**, Oakton Community College, IL; **Arlys Arnold**, University of Minnesota, MN; **Marcia Arthur**, Renton Technical College, WA; **Anne Bachmann**, Clackamas Community College, OR; **Ron Balsamo**, Santa Rosa Junior College, CA; **Lori Barkley**, Portland State University, OR; **Eileen Barlow**, SUNY Albany, NY; **Sue Bartch**, Cuyahoga Community College, OH; **Lora Bates**, Oakton High School, VA; **Nancy Baum**, University of Texas at Arlington, TX; **Linda Berendsen**, Oakton Community College, IL; **Jennifer Binckes Lee**, Howard Community College, MD; **Grace Bishop**, Houston Community College, TX; **Jean W. Bodman**, Union County College, NJ; **Virginia Bouchard**, George Mason University, VA; **Kimberley Briesch Sumner**, University of Southern California, CA; **Gabriela Cambiasso**, Harold Washington College, IL; **Jackie Campbell**, Capistrano Unified School District, CA; **Adele C. Camus**, George Mason University, VA; **Laura Chason**, Savannah College, GA; **Kerry Linder Catana**, Language Studies International, NY; **An Cheng**, Oklahoma State University, OK; **Carole Collins**, North Hampton Community College, PA; **Betty R. Compton**, Intercultural Communications College, HI; **Pamela Couch**, Boston University, MA; **Fernanda Crowe**, Intrax International Institute, CA; **Margo Czinski**, Washtenaw Community College, MI; **David Dahnke**, Lone Star College, TX; **Gillian M. Dale**, CA; **L. Dalgish**, Concordia College, MN; **Christopher Davis**, John Jay College, NY; **Sonia Delgadillo**, Sierra College, CA; **Marta O. Dmytrenko-Ahrabian**, Wayne State University, MI; **Javier Dominguez**, Central High School, SC; **Jo Ellen Downey-Greer**, Lansing Community College, MI; **Jennifer Duclos**, Boston University, MA; **Yvonne Duncan**, City College of San Francisco, CA; **Jennie Farnell**, University of Connecticut, CT; **Susan Fedors**, Howard Community College, MD; **Matthew Florence**, Intrax International Institute, CA; **Kathleen Flynn**, Glendale College, CA; **Eve Fonseca**, St. Louis Community College, MO; **Elizabeth Foss**, Washtenaw Community College, MI; **Duff C. Galda**, Pima Community College, AZ; **Christiane Galvani**, Houston Community College, TX; **Gretchen Gerber**, Howard Community College, MD; **Ray Gonzalez**, Montgomery College, MD; **Alyona Gorokhova**, Grossmont College, CA; **John Graney**, Santa Fe College, FL; **Kathleen Green**, Central High School, AZ; **Webb Hamilton**, De Anza College, San Jose City College, CA; **Janet Harclerode**, Santa Monica Community College, CA; **Sandra Hartmann**, Language and Culture Center, TX; **Kathy Haven**, Mission College, CA; **Adam Henricksen**, University of Maryland, MD; **Peter Hoffman**, LaGuardia Community College, NY; **Linda Holden**, College of Lake County, IL; **Jana Holt**, Lake Washington Technical College, WA; **Gail Ibele**, University of Wisconsin, WI; **Mandy Kama**, Georgetown University, Washington, DC; **Stephanie Kasuboski**, Cuyahoga Community College, OH; **Chigusa Katoku**, Mission College, CA; **Sandra Kawamura**, Sacramento City College, CA; **Gail Kellersberger**, University of Houston, TX; **Jane Kelly**, Durham Technical Community College, NC; **Julie Park Kim**, George Mason University, VA; **Lisa Kovacs-Morgan**, University of California, San Diego, CA; **Claudia Kupiec**, DePaul University, IL; **Renee La Rue**, Lone Star College-Montgomery, TX; **Janet Langon**, Glendale College, CA; **Lawrence Lawson**, Palomar College, CA; **Rachele Lawton**, The Community College of Baltimore County, MD; **Alice Lee**, Richland College, TX; **Cherie Lenz-Hackett**, University of Washington, WA; **Joy Leventhal**, Cuyahoga Community College, OH; **Candace Lynch-Thompson**, North Orange County Community College District, CA; **Thi Thi Ma**, City College of San Francisco, CA; **Denise Maduli-Williams**, City College of San Francisco, CA; **Eileen Mahoney**, Camelback High School, AZ; **Brigitte Maronde**, Harold Washington College, IL; **Keith Maurice**, University of Texas at Arlington, TX; **Nancy Mayer**, University of Missouri-St. Louis, MO; **Karen Merritt**, Grossmont Union High School District, CA; **Holly Milkowart**, Johnson County Community College, KS; **Eric Moyer**, Intrax International Institute, CA; **Gino Muzzatti**, Santa Rosa Junior College, CA; **William Nedrow**, Triton College, IL; **Eric Nelson**, University of Minnesota, MN; **Rhony Ory**, Ygnacio Valley High School, CA; **Paul Parent**, Montgomery College, MD; **Oscar Pedroso**, Miami Dade College, FL; **Robin Persiani**, Sierra College, CA; **Patricia Prenz-Belkin**,

Hostos Community College, NY; **Jim Ranalli**, Iowa State University, IA; **Toni R. Randall**, Santa Monica College, CA; **Vidya Rangachari**, Mission College, CA; **Elizabeth Rasmussen**, Northern Virginia Community College, VA; **Lara Ravitch**, Truman College, IL; **Deborah Repasz**, San Jacinto College, TX; **Andrey Reznikov**, Black Hills State University, SD; **Alison Rice**, Hunter College, NY; **Jennifer Robles**, Ventura Unified School District, CA; **Priscilla Rocha**, Clark County School District, NV; **Dzidra Rodins**, DePaul University IL; **Maria Rodriguez**, Central High School, AZ; **Maria Ruiz**, Victor Valley College, CA; **Kimberly Russell**, Clark College, WA; **Irene Sakk**, Northwestern University, IL; **Shaeley Santiago**, Ames High School, IA; **Peg Sarosy**, San Francisco State University, CA; **Alice Savage**, North Harris College, TX; **Donna Schaeffer**, University of Washington, WA; **Carol Schinger**, Northern Virginia Community College, VA; **Robert Scott**, Kansas State University, KA; **Suell Scott**, Sheridan Technical Center, FL; **Shira Seaman**, Global English Academy, NY; **Richard Seltzer**, Glendale Community College, CA; **Kathy Sherak**, San Francisco State University, CA; **German Silva**, Miami Dade College, FL; **Andrea Spector**, Santa Monica Community College, CA; **Karen Stanely**, Central Piedmont Community College, NC; **Ayse Stromsdorfer**, Soldan I.S.H.S., MO; **Yilin Sun**, South Seattle Community College, WA; **Thomas Swietlik**, Intrax International Institute, IL; **Judith Tanka**, UCLA Extension–American Language Center, CA; **Priscilla Taylor**, University of Southern California, CA; **Ilene Teixeira**, Fairfax County Public Schools, VA; **Shirl H. Terrell**, Collin College, TX; **Marya Teutsch-Dwyer**, St. Cloud State University, MN; **Stephen Thergesen**, ELS Language Centers, CO; **Christine Tierney**, Houston Community College, TX; **Arlene Turini**, North Moore High School, NC; **Suzanne Van Der Valk**, Iowa State University, IA; **Nathan D. Vasarhely**, Ygnacio Valley High School, CA; **Naomi S. Verratti**, Howard Community College, MD; **Hollyahna Vettori**, Santa Rosa Junior College, CA; **Laura Walsh**, City College of San Francisco, CA; **Andrew J. Watson**, The English Bakery; **Donald Weasenforth**, Collin College, TX; **Juliane Widner**, Sheepshead Bay High School, NY; **Lynne Wilkins**, Mills College, CA; **Dolores "Lorrie" Winter**, California State University at Fullerton, CA; **Jody Yamamoto**, Kapiʻolani Community College, HI; **Ellen L. Yaniv**, Boston University, MA; **Norman Yoshida**, Lewis & Clark College, OR; **Joanna Zadra**, American River College, CA; **Florence Zysman**, Santiago Canyon College, CA;

ASIA Rabiatu Abubakar, Eton Language Centre, Malaysia; **Wiwik Andreani**, Bina Nusantara University, Indonesia; **Mike Baker**, Kosei Junior High School, Japan; **Leonard Barrow**, Kanto Junior College, Japan; **Herman Bartelen**, Japan; **Siren Betty**, Fooyin University, Kaohsiung; **Thomas E. Bieri**, Nagoya College, Japan; **Natalie Brezden**, Global English House, Japan; **MK Brooks**, Mukogawa Women's University, Japan; **Truong Ngoc Buu**, The Youth Language School, Vietnam; **Charles Cabell**, Toyo University, Japan; **Fred Carruth**, Matsumoto University, Japan; **Frances Causer**, Seijo University, Japan; **Deborah Chang**, Wenzao Ursuline College of Languages, Kaohsiung; **David Hindman Chatham**, Ritsumeikan University, Japan; **Andrew Chih Hong Chen**, National Sun Yat-sen University, Kaohsiung; **Christina Chen**, Yu-Tsai Bilingual Elementary School, Taipei; **Jason Jeffree Cole**, Coto College, Japan; **Le Minh Cong**, Vungtau Tourism Vocational College, Vietnam; **Todd Cooper**, Toyama National College of Technology, Japan; **Marie Cosgrove**, Daito Bunka University, Japan; **Tony Cripps**, Ritsumeikan University, Japan; **Daniel Cussen**, Takushoku University, Japan; **Le Dan**, Ho Chi Minh City Electric Power College, Vietnam; **Simon Daykin**, Banghwa-dong Community Centre, South Korea; **Aimee Denham**, ILA, Vietnam; **Bryan Dickson**, David's English Center, Taipei; **Nathan Ducker**, Japan University, Japan; **Ian Duncan**, Simul International Corporate Training, Japan; **Nguyen Thi Kieu Dung**, Thang Long University, Vietnam; **Nguyen Thi Thuy Duong**, Vietnamese American Vocational Training College, Vietnam; **Wong Tuck Ee**, Raja Tun Azlan Science Secondary School, Malaysia; **Emilia Effendy**, International Islamic University Malaysia, Malaysia; **Robert Eva**, Kaisei Girls High School, Japan; **Jim George**, Luna International Language School, Japan; **Jurgen Germeys**, Silk Road Language Center, South Korea; **Wong Ai Gnoh**, SMJK Chung Hwa Confucian, Malaysia; **Peter Gooselink**, Hokkai High School,

Japan; **Wendy M. Gough**, St. Mary College/Nunoike Gaigo Senmon Gakko, Japan; **Tim Grose**, Sapporo Gakuin University, Japan; **Pham Thu Ha**, Le Van Tam Primary School, Vietnam; **Ann-Marie Hadzima**, Taipei; **Troy Hammond**, Tokyo Gakugei University International Secondary School, Japan; **Robiatul 'Adawiah Binti Hamzah**, SMK Putrajaya Precinct 8(1), Malaysia; **Tran Thi Thuy Hang**, Ho Chi Minh City Banking University, Vietnam; **To Thi Hong Hanh**, CEFALT, Vietnam; **Janis Hearn**, Hongik University, South Korea; **David Hindman**, Sejong University, South Korea; **Nahn Cam Hoa**, Ho Chi Minh City University of Technology, Vietnam; **Jana Holt**, Korea University, South Korea; **Jason Hollowell**, Nihon University, Japan; **F. N. (Zoe) Hsu**, National Tainan University, Yong Kang; **Wenhua Hsu**, I-Shou University, Kaohsiung; **Luu Nguyen Quoc Hung,** Cantho University, Vietnam ; **Cecile Hwang**, Changwon National University, South Korea; **Ainol Haryati Ibrahim**, Universiti Malaysia Pahang, Malaysia; **Robert Jeens**, Yonsei University, South Korea; **Linda M. Joyce**, Kyushu Sangyo University, Japan; **Dr. Nisai Kaewsanchai**, English Square Kanchanaburi, Thailand; **Aniza Kamarulzaman**, Sabah Science Secondary School, Malaysia; **Ikuko Kashiwabara**, Osaka Electro-Communication University, Japan; **Gurmit Kaur**, INTI College, Malaysia; **Nick Keane**, Japan; **Ward Ketcheson**, Aomori University, Japan; **Montchatry Ketmuni**, Rajamangala University of Technology, Thailand; **Dinh Viet Khanh**, Vietnam; **Seonok Kim**, Kangsu Jongro Language School, South Korea; **Kelly P. Kimura**, Soka University, Japan; **Stan Kirk**, Konan University, Japan; **Donald Knight**, Nan Hua/Fu Li Junior High Schools, Hsinchu; **Kari J. Kostiainen**, Nagoya City University, Japan; **Pattri Kuanpulpol**, Silpakorn University, Thailand; **Ha Thi Lan**, Thai Binh Teacher Training College, Vietnam; **Eric Edwin Larson**, Miyazaki Prefectural Nursing University, Japan; **Richard S. Lavin**, Prefectural University of Kumamoto, Japan; **Shirley Leane**, Chugoku Junior College, Japan; **Tae Lee**, Yonsei University, South Korea; **Lys Yongsoon Lee**, Reading Town Geumcheon, South Korea; **Mallory Leece**, Sun Moon University, South Korea; **Dang Hong Lien**, Tan Lam Upper Secondary School, Vietnam; **Huang Li-Han**, Rebecca Education Institute, Taipei; **Sovannarith Lim**, Royal University of Phnom Penh, Cambodia; **Ginger Lin**, National Kaohsiung Hospitality College, Kaohsiung; **Noel Lineker**, New Zealand/Japan; **Tran Dang Khanh Linh**, Nha Trang Teachers' Training College, Vietnam; **Daphne Liu**, Buliton English School, Taipei; **S. F. Josephine Liu**, Tien-Mu Elementary School, Taipei ; **Caroline Luo**, Tunghai University, Taichung; **Jeng-Jia Luo**, Tunghai University, Taichung; **Laura MacGregor**, Gakushuin University, Japan; **Amir Madani**, Visuttharangsi School, Thailand; **Elena Maeda**, Sacred Heart Professional Training College, Japan; **Vu Thi Thanh Mai**, Hoang Gia Education Center, Vietnam; **Kimura Masakazu**, Kato Gakuen Gyoshu High School, Japan; **Susumu Matsuhashi**, Net Link English School, Japan; **James McCrostie**, Daito Bunka University, Japan; **Joel McKee**, Inha University, South Korea; **Colin McKenzie**, Wachirawit Primary School, Thailand; **William K. Moore**, Hiroshima Kokusai Gakuin University, Japan; **Hudson Murrell**, Baiko Gakuin University, Japan; **Frances Namba**, Senri International School of Kwansei Gakuin, Japan; **Keiichi Narita**, Niigata University, Japan; **Kim Chung Nguyen**, Ho Chi Minh University of Industry, Vietnam; **Do Thi Thanh Nhan**, Hanoi University, Vietnam; **Dale Kazuo Nishi**, Aoyama English Conversation School, Japan; **Louise Ohashi**, Shukutoku University, Japan; **Virgina Peng**, Ritsumeikan University, Japan; **Suangkanok Piboonthamnont**, Rajamangala University of Technology, Thailand; **Simon Pitcher**, Business English Teaching Services, Japan; **John C. Probert**, New Education Worldwide, Thailand; **Do Thi Hoa Quyen**, Ton Duc Thang University, Vietnam; **John P. Racine**, Dokkyo University, Japan; **Kevin Ramsden**, Kyoto University of Foreign Studies, Japan; **Luis Rappaport**, Cung Thieu Nha Ha Noi, Vietnam; **Lisa Reshad**, Konan Daigaku Hyogo, Japan; **Peter Riley**, Taisho University, Japan; **Thomas N. Robb**, Kyoto Sangyo University, Japan; **Maria Feti Rosyani**, Universitas Kristen Indonesia, Indonesia; **Greg Rouault**, Konan University, Japan; **Chris Ruddenklau**, Kindai University, Japan; **Hans-Gustav Schwartz**, Thailand; **Mary-Jane Scott**, Soongsil University, South Korea; **Jenay Seymour,** Hongik University, South Korea; **James Sherlock**, A.P.W. Angthong, Thailand; **Yuko Shimizu**, Ritsumeikan University, Japan; **Suzila Mohd Shukor**, Universiti Sains Malaysia, Malaysia; **Stephen E. Smith**, Mahidol University, Thailand; **Mi-young Song**, Kyungwon University, South Korea; **Jason Stewart**, Taejon International Language School, South Korea; **Brian A. Stokes,** Korea University, South Korea; **Mulder Su**, Shih-Chien University, Kaohsiung;

Yoomi Suh, English Plus, South Korea; **Yun-Fang Sun**, Wenzao Ursuline College of Languages, Kaohsiung; **Richard Swingle**, Kansai Gaidai University, Japan; **Tran Hoang Tan**, School of International Training, Vietnam; **Takako Tanaka**, Doshisha University, Japan; **Jeffrey Taschner**, American University Alumni Language Center, Thailand ; **Michael Taylor**, International Pioneers School, Thailand; **Tran Duong The**, Sao Mai Language Center, Vietnam; **Tran Dinh Tho**, Duc Tri Secondary School, Vietnam; **Huynh Thi Anh Thu**, Nhatrang College of Culture Arts and Tourism, Vietnam; **Peter Timmins**, Peter's English School, Japan; **Fumie Togano**, Hosei Daini High School, Japan; **F. Sigmund Topor**, Keio University Language School, Japan; **Yen-Cheng Tseng**, Chang-Jung Christian University, Tainan; **Hajime Uematsu**, Hirosaki University, Japan; **Rachel Um**, Mok-dong Oedae English School, South Korea; **David Underhill**, EEExpress, Japan; **Siriluck Usaha**, Sripatum University, Thailand; **Tyas Budi Utami**, Indonesia; **Nguyen Thi Van**, Far East International School, Vietnam; **Stephan Van Eycken**, Kosei Gakuen Girls High School, Japan; **Zisa Velasquez**, Taihu International School/Semarang International School, China/Indonesia; **Jeffery Walter**, Sangji University, South Korea; **Bill White**, Kinki University, Japan; **Yohanes De Deo Widyastoko**, Xaverius Senior High School, Indonesia; **Greg Chung-Hsien Wu**, Providence University, Taichung; **Hui-Lien Yeh**, Chai Nan University of Pharmacy and Science, Tainan; **Sittiporn Yodnil**, Huachiew Chalermprakiet University, Thailand; **Shamshul Helmy Zambahari**, Universiti Teknologi Malaysia, Malaysia; **Aimin Fadhlee bin Mahmud Zuhodi**, Kuala Terengganu Science School, Malaysia;

TURKEY **Seval Akmeşe**, Haliç University; **Gül Akkoç**, Boğaziçi University; **Deniz Balım**, Haliç University; **Robert Ledbury**, Izmir University of Economics; **Oya Özağaç**, Boğaziçi University;

THE MIDDLE EAST **Amina Saif Mohammed Al Hashamia**, Nizwa College of Applied Sciences, Oman; **Sharon Ruth Devaneson**, Ibri College of Technology, Oman; **Hanaa El-Deeb**, Canadian International College, Egypt; **Brian Gay**, Sultan Qaboos University, Oman; **Gail Al-Hafidh**, Sharjah Higher Colleges of Technology, U.A.E.; **Jonathan Hastings**, American Language Center, Jordan; **Sian Khoury**, Fujairah Women's College (HCT), U.A.E.; **Jessica March**, American University of Sharjah, U.A.E.; **Neil McBeath**, Sultan Qaboos University, Oman;

LATIN AMERICA **Aldana Aguirre**, Argentina; **Claudia Almeida**, Coordenação de Idiomas, Brazil; **Cláudia Arias**, Brazil; **Maria de los Angeles Barba**, FES Acatlan UNAM, Mexico; **Lilia Barrios**, Universidad Autónoma de Tamaulipas, Mexico; **Adán Beristain**, UAEM, Mexico; **Ricardo Böck**, Manoel Ribas, Brazil; **Edson Braga**, CNA, Brazil; **Marli Buttelli**, Mater et Magistra, Brazil; **Alessandra Campos**, Inova Centro de Linguas, Brazil; **Priscila Catta Preta Ribeiro**, Brazil; **Gustavo Cestari**, Access International School, Brazil; **Walter D'Alessandro**, Virginia Language Center, Brazil; **Lilian De Gennaro**, Argentina; **Mônica De Stefani**, Quality Centro de Idiomas, Brazil; **Julio Alejandro Flores**, BUAP, Mexico; **Mirian Freire**, CNA Vila Guilherme, Brazil; **Francisco Garcia**, Colegio Lestonnac de San Angel, Mexico; **Miriam Giovanardi**, Brazil; **Darlene Gonzalez Miy**, ITESM CCV, Mexico; **Maria Laura Grimaldi**, Argentina; **Luz Dary Guzmán**, IMPAHU, Colombia; **Carmen Koppe**, Brazil; **Monica Krutzler**, Brazil; **Marcus Murilo Lacerda**, Seven Idiomas, Brazil; **Nancy Lake**, CEL-LEP, Brazil; **Cris Lazzerini**, Brazil; **Sandra Luna**, Argentina; **Ricardo Luvisan**, Brazil; **Jorge Murilo Menezes**, ACBEU, Brazil; **Monica Navarro**, Instituto Cultural A. C., Mexico; **Joacyr Oliveira**, Faculdades Metropolitanas Unidas and Summit School for Teachers, Brazil; **Ayrton Cesar Oliveira de Araujo**, E&A English Classes, Brazil; **Ana Laura Oriente**, Seven Idiomas, Brazil; **Adelia Peña Clavel**, CELE UNAM, Mexico; **Beatriz Pereira**, Summit School, Brazil; **Miguel Perez**, Instituto Cultural Mexico; **Cristiane Perone**, Associação Cultura Inglesa, Brazil; **Pamela Claudia Pogré**, Colegio Integral Caballito/ Universidade de Flores, Argentina; **Dalva Prates**, Brazil; **Marianne Rampaso**, Iowa Idiomas, Brazil; **Daniela Rutolo**, Instituto Superior Cultural Británico, Argentina; **Maione Sampaio**, Maione Carrijo Consultoria em Inglês Ltda, Brazil; **Elaine Santesso**, TS Escola de Idiomas, Brazil; **Camila Francisco Santos**, UNS Idiomas, Brazil; **Lucia Silva**, Cooplem Idiomas, Brazil; **Maria Adela Sorzio**, Instituto Superior Santa Cecilia, Argentina; **Elcio Souza**, Unibero, Brazil; **Willie Thomas**, Rainbw Idiomas, Brazil; **Sandra Villegas**, Instituto Humberto de Paolis, Argentina; **John Whelan**, La Universidad Nacional Autonoma de Mexico, Mexico

WELCOME TO Q:Skills for Success

Q: Skills for Success is a six-level series with two strands,
Reading and Writing and *Listening and Speaking*.

READING AND WRITING

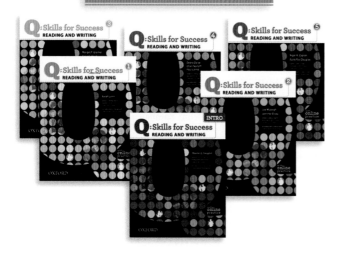

LISTENING AND SPEAKING

WITH Q ONLINE PRACTICE

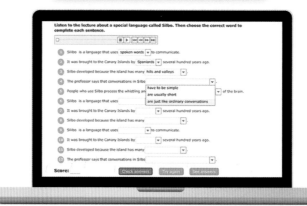

STUDENT AND TEACHER INFORMED

Q: Skills for Success is the result of an extensive development process involving thousands of teachers and hundreds of students around the world. Their views and opinions helped shape the content of the series. *Q* is grounded in teaching theory as well as real-world classroom practice, making it the most learner-centered series available.

CONTENTS

Q connects critical thinking, language skills, and learning outcomes.

LANGUAGE SKILLS

Explicit skills instruction enables students to meet their academic and professional goals.

LEARNING OUTCOMES

Clearly identified **learning outcomes** focus students on the goal of their instruction.

UNIT 9

Numbers

READING ● making inferences
VOCABULARY ● numbers and mathematical terms
WRITING ● using numbers to support ideas
GRAMMAR ● the present perfect

LEARNING OUTCOME ●
Describe your personal experience of learning math in a paragraph that includes numbers and facts.

 Unit QUESTION

Does everyone need math?

PREVIEW THE UNIT

A Discuss these questions with your classmates.

Do you like or dislike doing math? Why?

Can you think of any jobs that don't use math?

Look at the photo. How is this person using math?

B Discuss the Unit Question above with your classmates.

Listen to *The Q Classroom*, Track 11 on CD 2, to hear other answers.

162 UNIT 9

163

CRITICAL THINKING

Thought-provoking **unit questions** engage students with the topic and provide a **critical thinking framework** for the unit.

 Having the learning outcome is important because it gives students and teachers a clear idea of what the point of each task/activity in the unit is.
Lawrence Lawson, Palomar College, California

Cultural Differences in Counting

1 How quickly can you count from one to ten? Do you use ten different words to do it? Can you do it in English, or do you have to use your first language? Do you count on your fingers? Many people **assume** that numbers and math are the same all over the world. But scientists have discovered that this is not true.

2 People in different parts of the world use different **methods** to count on their fingers. In the United States, people begin counting with their first, or index, finger, which they

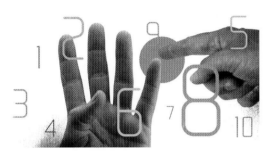

extend or stick out. They then extend the rest of their fingers and finally the thumb to count to five. Then they repeat this with the other hand to get to ten. In some cultures, people begin with their fingers already extended. They count by folding the fingers inward. In China, people count by using a variety of finger positions. In this way, a Chinese person can easily count to ten on only one hand, while an American uses two hands to count to ten.

3 In addition to methods of finger counting, scientists have found that cultures and languages also differ when it comes to numbers. Some languages have only a few words for numbers, and others don't have any words for numbers. A group of scientists worked with aboriginal[1] children in Australia. The scientists studied people who have a very small vocabulary for numbers. Unlike many groups, these people don't have gestures or hand movements to **indicate** numbers. In most cultures, people count on fingers to indicate a number, but not in these aboriginal tribes[2].

Q WHAT DO YOU THINK?

Discuss the questions in a group. Then choose one question and write five to eight sentences in response.

1. What was the most surprising thing that you learned in this article?

2. The Pirahã tribe and the aboriginal people in Australia don't really seem to need numbers. What kinds of things do you use numbers for in your daily life? Can you imagine a day without numbers? Why or why not?

One of the best features is your focus on developing materials of a high "interest level."
Troy Hammond, Tokyo Gakugei University, International Secondary School, Japan

Explicit skills instruction prepares students for academic success.

LANGUAGE SKILLS

Explicit instruction and practice in reading, vocabulary, grammar and writing skills **help students achieve language proficiency.**

LEARNING OUTCOMES

Practice activities allow students to **master the skills** before they are evaluated at the end of the unit.

_____ 4. In tests, aboriginal children had to match pictures with numbers.

_____ 5. The scientists who went to Brazil were from the California Institute of Technology.

_____ 6. The Pirahã tribe are aboriginal people in Australia.

_____ 7. The Pirahã don't have words for precise numbers.

_____ 8. The tribes in the study live in urban areas.

_____ 9. The Pirahã have a word that can mean "one" or "two."

_____ 10. The Pirahã need to use numbers in their everyday lives.

WHAT DO YOU THINK?

Discuss the questions in a group. Then choose one question and write five to eight sentences in response.

1. What was the most surprising thing that you learned in this article?

2. The Pirahã tribe and the aboriginal people in Australia don't really seem to need numbers. What kinds of things do you use numbers for in your daily life? Can you imagine a day without numbers? Why or why not?

| Reading Skill | Making inferences |  |

When you make an **inference** about a text, you determine that something is true even though the writer does not tell you directly.

Suzy yawned as she tried to keep her eyes open.

You can **infer** that Suzy was tired, even though the writer didn't say, "Suzy was tired." You can infer this because usually when people yawn and can't keep their eyes open, they are tired. However, you can't infer that she stayed up all night. There are no clues in the text to suggest this, and there are many reasons she could be tired.

To make inferences, use clues from the text and your own knowledge and experience to figure out what the author is trying to tell you. Making inferences is a useful skill because it's a way to gain a deeper understanding of the text. It is sometimes called "reading between the lines."

Reading and Writing **169**

WRITING

| Writing Skill | Using numbers to support ideas | |

When you write a paragraph, you can use facts to support your ideas. Using **numbers** and **facts** can make your ideas even stronger and more interesting. You can use sources such as books, magazines, and online articles to find numerical facts that support your ideas.

This year, the winter was much colder than usual. This winter's average temperature was **five degrees** below the usual average.

Many people support the president. Currently, **65 percent of the people** think he is doing a good job.

Investments in the stock market have increased. People invested **more than $5 billion** last year.

A. Read the paragraph. Then answer the questions.

> The population of the world is increasing at a dangerous rate. In 1810, the world's population was about one billion people. That figure doubled by 1930. The population reached three billion by 1965, four billion by 1975, and five billion by 1990. By the year 2000, the earth's population was more than six billion people. If the population continues to grow at this rate, the earth may run out of food and water for all of the people who live here.

1. What is the main idea of the paragraph?

_____

2. What happened in 1930?

_____

3. What kinds of numbers and facts does the writer use to support his ideas?

_____
_____

4. What numbers or information might be helpful to support the idea in the last sentence of the paragraph?

_____
_____

178 **UNIT 9** Does everyone need math?

 The tasks are simple, accessible, user-friendly, and very useful.
Jessica March, American University of Sharjah, U.A.E.

Q Online Practice provides all new content for additional practice in an easy-to-use online workbook. Every student book includes a *Q Online Practice access code card*. Use the access code to register for your *Q Online Practice* account at www.Qonlinepractice.com.

Vocabulary Skill | **Using the dictionary**

Words with more than one meaning

Many words have more than one meaning, or definition, even if they are spelled and pronounced the same way. Using a dictionary can help you identify the correct meaning of a new word. If a word has two definitions that are the same part of speech (*noun, verb, adjective, adverb*), they will appear under the same entry in the dictionary. If the two meanings are different parts of speech, they will appear under different entries in the dictionary.

light¹ /laɪt/ *noun* **1** [C, U] the energy from the sun, a lamp, etc. that allows you to see things: *a beam/ray of light* ◆ *the light of the sun* ◆ *The light was too bad for us to read by.* **2** [C] something that produces light, for example an electric lamp: *Suddenly, all the lights came on/went out.* ◆ *the lights of the city in the distance* ◆ *a neon light* ◆ *That car's lights aren't on.* ◆ *Please switch the lights off before you leave.*

light² /laɪt/ *adj.*
➤ NOT DARK **1** having a lot of light: *In the summer it's still light at 9 o'clock.* ◆ *a light room* **ANT** **dark**
➤ OF A COLOR **2** pale in color: *a light blue sweater* **ANT** **dark**
➤ NOT HEAVY **3** not of great weight: *Carry this bag – it's the lightest.* ◆ *I've lost weight – I'm five pounds lighter than I used to be.* ◆ *light clothes* (= for summer) **ANT** **heavy**

All dictionary entries are taken from the *Oxford American Dictionary for learners of English.*

A **research-based vocabulary program** focuses students on the words they need to know academically and professionally, using skill strategies based on the same research as the Oxford dictionaries.

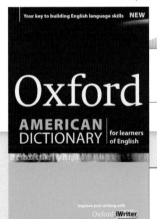

All dictionary entries are taken from the *Oxford American Dictionary for learners of English.*

The *Oxford American Dictionary for learners of English* was developed with English learners in mind, and provides extra learning tools for pronunciation, verb types, basic grammar structures, and more.

The Oxford 3000™
The Oxford 3000 encompasses **the 3000 most important words to learn in English.** It is based on a comprehensive analysis of the Oxford English Corpus, a two billion word collection of English text, and on extensive research with both language and pedagogical experts.

The Academic Word List **AWL**
The Academic Word List was created by Averil Coxhead and contains **570 words that are commonly used in academic English,** such as in textbooks or articles across a wide range of academic subject areas. These words are a great place to start if you are studying English for academic purposes.

Clear learning outcomes focus students on the goals of instruction.

LEARNING OUTCOMES

A culminating unit assignment evaluates the students' **mastery of the learning outcome.**

Unit Assignment | **Write a paragraph using numbers to support ideas**

In this assignment you will write a paragraph about your personal experience of learning math and use numbers to support your ideas. As you prepare your paragraph, think about the Unit Question, "Does everyone need math?" and refer to the Self-Assessment checklist on page 182.

For alternative unit assignments, see the *Q: Skills for Success Teacher's Handbook.*

PLAN AND WRITE

A. BRAINSTORM Think about your experience learning math. Write your positive and negative experiences learning math in the T-chart below.

Positive experiences	Negative experiences

LEARNER CENTERED

Track Your Success allows students to **assess their own progress** and provides guidance on remediation.

Check (✓) the skills you learned. If you need more work on a skill, refer to the pages in parentheses.

READING	○	I can make inferences. (p. 169)
VOCABULARY	○	I can use numbers and mathematical terms. (p. 176)
WRITING	○	I can use numbers to support ideas. (p. 178)
GRAMMAR	○	I can use the present perfect. (p. 179)
LEARNING OUTCOME	○	I can describe my personal experience of learning math in a paragraph that includes numbers and facts.

Students can check their learning ... and they can focus on the essential points when they study.

Suh Yoomi, Seoul, South Korea

For the student

- **Easy-to-use:** a simple interface allows students to focus on enhancing their speaking and listening skills, not learning a new software program
- **Flexible:** for use anywhere there's an Internet connection
- **Access code card:** a *Q Online Practice* access code is included with this book—use the access code to register for *Q Online Practice* at www.Qonlinepractice.com

For the teacher

- **Simple yet powerful:** automatically grades student exercises and tracks progress
- **Straightforward:** online management system to review, print, or export the reports they need
- **Flexible:** for use in the classroom or easily assigned as homework
- **Access code card:** contact your sales rep for your *Q Online Practice* teacher's access code

Teacher Resources

Q Teacher's Handbook gives strategic support through:

- specific teaching notes for each activity
- ideas for ensuring student participation
- multilevel strategies and expansion activities
- the answer key
- special sections on 21st Century Skills and critical thinking
- a *Testing Program CD-ROM* with a customizable test for each unit

Oxford
Teachers' Club

For additional resources visit the
Q: Skills for Success companion website at
www.oup.com/elt/teacher/Qskillsforsuccess

Q Class Audio includes:

- listening texts
- pronunciation presentations and exercises
- *The Q Classroom*

It's an interesting, engaging series which provides plenty of materials that are easy to use in class, as well as instructionally promising.
Donald Weasenforth, Collin College, Texas

UNIT	READING	WRITING
1 Trends **Why does something become popular?** **READING 1:** The Popularity of Social Networks An online article (Marketing) **READING 2:** A Song Becomes a Hit A Magazine Article (Music)	• Preview text using a variety of strategies • Read for main ideas • Read for details • Activate schema with photos/pictures • Use glosses and footnotes to aid comprehension • Read and recognize different text types • Make predictions before reading • Order ideas to recognize sequence	• Write paragraphs of different genres • Plan before writing • Revise, edit, and rewrite • Give feedback to peers and self • Write a topic sentence to convey ideas clearly • Write a descriptive paragraph
2 Color **How do colors affect the way we feel?** **READING 1:** How Colors Make Us Think and Feel A Textbook Article (Psychology) **READING 2:** The Importance of Color in Business A Magazine Article (Marketing)	• Preview text using a variety of strategies • Read for main ideas • Read for details • Activate schema with photos/pictures • Use glosses and footnotes to aid comprehension • Read and recognize different text types • Use context to understand unfamiliar words while reading • Complete a chart to organize information from reading	• Write paragraphs of different genres • Plan before writing • Revise, edit, and rewrite • Give feedback to peers and self • Use freewriting to brainstorm ideas before writing • Write a business proposal
3 Courtesy **What does it mean to be polite?** **READING 1:** Being Polite from Culture to Culture A Magazine Article (Interpersonal Communication) **READING 2:** Answers to All Your Travel Questions! An Online Discussion Group (Cultural Etiquette)	• Preview text using a variety of strategies • Read for main ideas • Read for details • Activate schema with photos/pictures • Use glosses and footnotes to aid comprehension • Read and recognize different text types • Identify supporting details to aid comprehension	• Write paragraphs of different genres • Plan before writing • Revise, edit, and rewrite • Give feedback to peers and self • Write a paragraph with supporting ideas • Complete a cluster diagram before writing • Write a paragraph

VOCABULARY	GRAMMAR	CRITICAL THINKING	UNIT OUTCOME
• Match definitions • Define new terms • Understand meaning from context • Distinguish word forms (nouns, verbs) to expand vocabulary	• Simple present and present continuous	• Reflect on the unit question • Connect ideas across texts or readings • Apply unit tips and Q online to be a strategic learner • Set and achieve goals • Support opinions with reasons • Complete a T-chart to categorize information	• Write a paragraph describing a current trend and why it is popular.
• Match definitions • Define new terms • Understand meaning from context • Learn suffixes to expand vocabulary • Complete a chart to identify word forms	• Conjunctions: *and, but, or, so*	• Reflect on the unit question • Connect ideas across texts or readings • Apply unit tips and Q online to be a strategic learner • Set and achieve goals • Relate information from reading to self	• Create a business and write a description explaining the colors you will use and why.
• Match definitions • Define new terms • Understand meaning from context • Learn prefixes to expand vocabulary • Complete a T-chart to categorize prefixes and suffixes	• Subect-verb agreement	• Reflect on the unit question • Connect ideas across texts or readings • Apply unit tips and Q online to be a strategic learner • Set and achieve goals • Support opinions with reasons or examples	• Write a paragraph in response to a question on an online discussion forum about politeness.

UNIT	READING	WRITING
4 Games **What makes a competition unfair?** **READING 1: Money and Sports** A Magazine Article (Sports) **READING 2: The Fastest Man on No Legs** A News Magazine Article (Ethics)	• Preview text using a variety of strategies • Read for main ideas • Read for details • Activate schema with photos/pictures • Use glosses and footnotes to aid comprehension • Read and recognize different text types • Read a chart to obtain information while reading • Take notes to retain information • Use a graphic organizer to categorize information from a reading	• Write paragraphs of different genres • Plan before writing • Revise, edit, and rewrite • Give feedback to peers and self • Use a cluster diagram to brainstorm ideas before writing • Write an opinion paragraph with supporting details
5 Family Ties **What makes a family business successful?** **READING 1: Family Unity Builds Success** A Magazine Article (Business) **READING 2: The Challenge of Running a Family Business** A Textbook Article (Business)	• Preview text using a variety of strategies • Read for main ideas • Read for details • Activate schema with photos/pictures • Use glosses and footnotes to aid comprehension • Read and recognize different text types • Skim a text quickly to get the general idea • Use a chart to compare information across readings	• Write paragraphs of different genres • Plan before writing • Revise, edit, and rewrite • Give feedback to peers and self • Write a personal letter using a standard format
6 Self-Reliance **Do you prefer to get help from a person or a machine?** **READING 1: Memo to Restaurant Servers** A Business Memo (Technology) **READING 2: I Hate Machines!** An Excerpt From a Blog (Opinion)	• Preview text using a variety of strategies • Read for main ideas • Read for details • Activate schema with photos/pictures • Use glosses and footnotes to aid comprehension • Read and recognize different text types • Identify the author's purpose for writing a text	• Write paragraphs of different genres • Plan before writing • Revise, edit, and rewrite • Give feedback to peers and self • Write a paragraph describing a process • Use time order words: *first, next, then, later, after that, finally*—to make steps in a process clear
7 Buy or Reuse **Is it better to save what you have or buy new things?** **READING 1: Think Before You Toss** A Magazine Article (Consumerism) **READING 2: In Praise of the Throwaway Society** A Blog (Opinion)	• Preview text using a variety of strategies • Read for main ideas • Read for details • Activate schema with photos/pictures • Use glosses and footnotes to aid comprehension • Read and recognize different text types • Distinguish between fact and opinion to read critically	• Write paragraphs of different genres • Plan before writing • Revise, edit, and rewrite • Give feedback to peers and self • Vary sentence types to make writing more interesting • Write an answer to a test question

VOCABULARY	GRAMMAR	CRITICAL THINKING	UNIT OUTCOME
• Match definitions • Define new terms • Understand meaning from context • Use the dictionary to learn more about words—pronunciation, parts of speech, and related forms	• Modals: *should, should not, ought to*	• Reflect on the unit question • Connect ideas across texts or readings • Apply *Tips for Success* to be a strategic learner • Set and achieve goals • Support opinions with reasons, examples, or supporting details	• Express and support your opinion about what makes a competition unfair.
• Match definitions • Define new terms • Understand meaning from context • Use the dictionary to learn more about words—count/noncount nouns, irregular forms	• Comparative and superlative adjectives	• Reflect on the unit question • Connect ideas across texts or readings • Apply *Tips for Success* to be a strategic learner • Set and achieve goals • Support opinions with reasons and examples • Relate information from reading to self • Compare information using a chart	• Write a personal letter describing a new family business.
• Match definitions • Define new terms • Understand meaning from context • Use the dictionary to distinguish words with multiple meanings	• Infinitives of purpose • Time order words: *first, next, then, later, after that, finally*	• Reflect on the unit question • Connect ideas across texts or readings • Apply *Tips for Success* to be a strategic learner • Set and achieve goals • Support opinions with reasons and examples • Complete a chart to identify steps in a process	• Describe the steps of a process performed by either a person or a machine.
• Match definitions • Define new terms • Understand meaning from context • Recognize the features of phrasal verbs in order to use them correctly	• Future Time clauses	• Discuss advantages and disadvantages • Relate information from reading to self	• Respond to a test question by writing a paragraph that states and supports your opinion.

UNIT	READING	WRITING
8 Stories ❓ **What makes a good story?** **READING 1:** Nasreddin Hodja and the Candle A Turkish Folktale (Literature) **READING 2:** Writing a Short Story A Textbook Excerpt (Writing)	• Preview text using a variety of strategies • Read for main ideas • Read for details • Activate schema with photos/pictures • Use glosses and footnotes to aid comprehension • Read and recognize different text types • Summarize text to check comprehension	• Write paragraphs of different genres • Plan before writing • Revise, edit, and rewrite • Give feedback to peers and self • Write a narrative paragraph
9 Numbers ❓ **Does everyone need math?** **READING 1:** Cultural Differences in Counting A Science Report (Mathematics) **READING 2:** Problems with Math A Personal Essay (Narrative)	• Preview text using a variety of strategies • Read for main ideas • Read for details • Activate schema with photos/pictures • Use glosses and footnotes to aid comprehension • Read and recognize different text types • Make inferences using clues from text and background knowledge in order to read critically	• Write paragraphs of different genres • Plan before writing • Revise, edit, and rewrite • Give feedback to peers and self • Write a paragraph using numbers/figures to support ideas
10 Global Health ❓ **How can we prevent diseases?** **READING 1:** Flu FAQ (Frequently Asked Questions) An Online FAQ (Health) **READING 2:** More Than a Game A Magazine Article (Psychology)	• Preview text using a variety of strategies • Read for main ideas • Read for details • Activate schema with photos/pictures • Use glosses and footnotes to aid comprehension • Read and recognize different text types • Synthesize information from multiple sources to deepen understanding while reading • Complete a Venn diagram to find similarities and differences in text	• Write paragraphs of different genres • Plan before writing • Revise, edit, and rewrite • Give feedback to peers and self • Write a definition paragraph • Analyze the structure of definitions • Write an FAQ page

VOCABULARY	GRAMMAR	CRITICAL THINKING	UNIT OUTCOME
• Match definitions • Define new terms • Understand meaning from context • Recognize word connotations to aid reading comprehension and apply to writing	• Simple past and past continuous	• Support opinions with reasons • Relate information from reading to self	• Write a short story that includes a main character, setting, conflict, and resolution.
• Match definitions • Define new terms • Understand meaning from context • Use numbers and mathematical terms for academic and everyday applications	• Present perfect	• Support opinions with reasons • Relate information from reading to self • Use a T-chart to organize information	• Describe your personal experience of learning math in a paragraph that includes numbers and facts.
• Match definitions • Define new terms • Understand meaning from context • Learn verb + preposition collocations to expand vocabulary	• Adverbs of manner and degree	• Support opinions with reasons and examples • Relate information in reading to self • Complete a flow chart to display details	• Create a FAQ (Frequently Asked Questions) page about an illness that includes a definition of your topic.

UNIT 1

Trends

READING ●	identifying the main idea of a paragraph
VOCABULARY ●	word families
WRITING ●	writing a topic sentence
GRAMMAR ●	simple present and present continuous

LEARNING OUTCOME

Write a paragraph describing a current trend and why it is popular.

Unit QUESTION

Why does something become popular?

PREVIEW THE UNIT

A Discuss these questions with your classmates.

How often do you use the Internet? What websites do you visit?

How do you find new music that you like?

Look at the photo. What is the woman doing?

B Discuss the Unit Question above with your classmates.

Listen to *The Q Classroom*, Track 2 on CD 1, to hear other answers.

3

C Read about social networking websites. Then put a check (✓) next to the photo that shows one.

The word *social* refers to the way that people connect or relate to each other. The word *network* refers to a system that connects computer users. A *social network* is a website that lets people connect and communicate with each other.

1

2

D Read the questionnaire below and answers the questions. Then interview a partner. Write your partner's answers in the questionnaire.

How Connected Are You?

Question	My answers	Partner's answers
1. How much time do you spend on the Internet each day?		
2. What do you do on the Internet?		
3. Are you part of a social network such as Facebook? If yes, which one?		
4. How much time do you spend on social networking sites every day?		
5. How do you usually listen to music? Do you buy and download music?		
6. What are some of your favorite songs? Are they popular now?		

READING 1 | The Popularity of Social Networks

VOCABULARY

Here are some words from Reading 1. Read their definitions. Then complete each sentence.

> **clear** (*adj.*) easy to see, hear, or understand
> **connected to** (*phr.*) joined or linked to something or someone
> **contribute** (*v.*) to give or be a part of something with other people
> **express** (*v.*) to say or show how you think or feel
> **find out** (*v.*) to get or discover information about something
> **keep in touch** (*v.*) to meet, call, or write someone often
> **spread** (*v.*) to affect a large area or group of people
> **trend** (*n.*) a change to something different

1. I don't know what time the concert starts. I'll go online and

   _____find out_____.

2. Many Americans are buying smaller cars that use less gas. They are part of

   a _____ that started a few years ago.

3. A small fire can _____ quickly in a dry place.

4. Each member of the group should _____ equally to the project.

5. Thanks to the Internet, Jean is always _____ her family,

   even though they live far away.

6. Because Doug and Liz don't speak Spanish well, they couldn't

   _____ themselves well when on vacation in Spain.

7. It's great to talk to my old school friends. We use email to

   _____.

8. It was very _____ that Noriko didn't do her homework.

   She didn't know any answers during the class discussion.

PREVIEW READING 1

This is an online article about the growing popularity of social networking websites. The article gives an example of a typical user named Sarah.

What do you think the article will say about why social networking websites are popular? Check (✓) your answers.

☐ because people like to connect with each other
☐ because the websites are free to use
☐ because people enjoy using computers

 CD 1 Track 3 **Read the online article.**

The Popularity of Social Networks

1   Every morning Sarah turns on her computer. First, she checks her email. Then, she visits a social networking website to find out what her friends are doing. On this website, she reads news from her friends. For example, she may look at comments her friends made about movies, music, books, and other friends. On her profile page, Sarah writes a short message about what she is doing. Like many young people, Sarah enjoys meeting and communicating with others on social networks. These websites let people see what their friends are doing and thinking.

2   Sarah is part of an important **trend** in communication. Social networking sites become more and more popular every day, and they are popular all around the world. In Japan, the top site is Mixi.

Useful Internet Terms

blog – a website where people write about things they are interested in. Others can leave comments about their writing.

chat – to communicate instantly with a group of people on the Internet

comments – short notes that you write to give your opinion or feeling about something

instant messaging – a way to communicate with one person instantly over the Internet

interactive– allowing direct two-way communication

link – a word or group of words on a website (often underlined) that you click to take you to a different website

online – to be connected to the Internet

post – to leave a message on a website where everyone can see it

site – short for website

In Europe, it is Bebo. The most popular site in Latin America is Orkut. In the United States, the top site is Facebook. In fact, Facebook is one of the most popular social networking sites in the world. A Harvard University student started Facebook in 2004, and it **spread** to more than 400 million users in just a few years.

3   Why is the social networking trend spreading so rapidly? One reason that these websites are popular is because people are social. We like to communicate with other people. We make friends with people in school, at work, and online. Most people like to stay closely **connected to** their friends and family. We use cell phones, email, instant messaging, and websites to learn what our friends are doing. The Internet is a good way to socialize and communicate, and social networking sites allow people to do this in many ways.

4   Social networking sites are interactive and personal. People can share photographs of themselves and of others. They can tell people what they are doing at any moment and **keep in touch**. They can post a link to a site with their favorite song or band. They can join groups with others who share their interests. Many people post videos of themselves on sites like YouTube. Other users can comment on these photos and videos. This interaction makes these websites become more popular.

5   Another reason that social networking sites are popular is because the users write what is on the site. In the past, websites only had information for users to read. In this way,

People can share photos of themselves on social networking sites.

websites were like newspapers or television. All of the communication went in only one direction: from the website to the users. In the past, the average person didn't **contribute** to the websites. Today, the Internet is more interactive than it was in the past. Now anyone can have their own website, blog, or page on sites like Facebook. Readers are now also writers and can easily add material to the Web. People can **express** their own ideas, and they can put their own experiences online.

6   Social networking sites first became popular with college students. At one college, students said that they spent almost two hours every day just on Facebook. Teenagers also use these sites to stay connected with their friends. These days, even older people are using social networks. The Internet keeps changing, but one trend is **clear**: People enjoy using websites that let them connect with others. They like to express themselves and communicate online.

MAIN IDEAS

A. Read the statements. Write *T* (true) or *F* (false).

_T_ 1. On social networking sites, people can see what their friends are doing and thinking.

___ 2. Social networking websites are popular only in the United States.

___ 3. Most people are not very social.

___ 4. Today, people can express their own ideas online.

___ 5. It is harder now for people to express themselves on the Internet.

___ 6. Social networking sites are popular with people of all ages.

Tip Critical Thinking

Activity B asks you to put the sentences **in order** (what happens first, second, third, and so on). **Ordering** is one way to show you understand the ideas in a reading.

B. Read the sentences. Then number them in the order that the information appears in the article.

___ a. Websites are more popular when people can share information about themselves.

___ b. Social networking sites become more and more popular every day.

___ c. Social networking sites first became popular with college students.

___ d. People like to stay closely connected to their friends and family.

___ e. The Internet keeps changing.

_1_ f. Social networks let people see what their friends are doing and thinking.

___ g. Today the Internet is more interactive than it was in the past.

DETAILS

Answer these questions.

1. What are two ways to communicate instantly online?

   _____chat_____ _____

2. What's the most popular social networking site in Japan? In Latin America?

   _____ _____

3. When did Facebook start? _____

4. What's the name of a popular site where users can post videos?

_____

5. Who can create their own website or blog? _____

 ## WHAT DO YOU THINK?

Discuss these questions in a group. Then choose one question and write five to eight sentences in response.

1. Which social networking sites are popular with your friends? Are they popular because of any of the reasons mentioned in Reading 1? If yes, which reasons?

2. Do you think that social networking sites are a good way to communicate with friends? Why or why not?

3. Think of a popular trend in technology. What is it? Are you part of that trend? Why or why not?

| Reading Skill | Identifying the main idea of a paragraph | |

A **paragraph** is a group of sentences about one topic. The **main idea** of a paragraph is the most important point about the topic. You can often find the main idea in the first or second sentence of a paragraph. This is the **topic sentence**. The other sentences help explain or support the main idea. Identifying the main idea of a paragraph will help you to understand and remember what you read.

A. Read the paragraphs. Then underline the main ideas.

1.   It's easy to keep in touch with people on the Internet. You can email friends and family. Many people can get free email accounts in just a few minutes. You can chat online. This is an easy way to communicate with someone right away. Another way to stay connected is on social networking sites. Social networking sites let you keep in touch with many people at once in a very short amount of time.

2.   Social networking sites are part of a very popular trend, especially with young people. Young adults in their mid-20s, however, often spend less time on social networking sites than teenagers. For teenagers, being connected with their peers is very important, and teenagers spend many hours online. During college, social networking sites often become less important. This may be because students see each other often and can easily get together. After college, young adults find jobs. In their mid-20s, they are busy and don't have as much free time for social networking sites.

B. Read the questions. Look back at Reading 1. Circle the correct answer for each question. Then underline the sentence in Reading 1 that helped you find the answer.

1. What is the main idea of paragraph 2?
   a. Today the Internet is more interactive than it was in the past.
   b. Social networking sites are popular.
   c. Sarah is part of an important trend in communication.

2. What is the main idea of paragraph 3?
   a. Websites are popular because people are social.
   b. People like to communicate with other people.
   c. Cell phones are a good way to communicate.

3. What is the main idea of paragraph 4?
   a. Social networking sites are a good place to share photographs online.
   b. Social networking sites are popular because they are interactive and personal.
   c. YouTube is a popular place to post videos on the Internet.

4. What is the main idea of paragraph 5?
   a. In the past, users could only read information on the Internet.
   b. Anyone can have a website or a page on Facebook.
   c. Social networking sites are popular because users write the information on the sites.

5. What's the main idea of paragraph 6?
   a. Social networking is popular only with teens.
   b. Social networking is popular with people of all ages.
   c. Adults don't use social networking sites.

READING 2 | A Song Becomes a Hit

VOCABULARY

Here are some words from Reading 2. Read the sentences. Then circle the answer that best matches the meaning of each bold word or phrase.

1. The new movie was a big **hit**. Every night the theater was full.
   a. loud sound
   b. popular success *(circled)*

2. Good advertisements can **influence** what we decide to buy.
   a. have an effect on
   b. delay

3. I was angry when I heard that Mia had **made up** the story about the accident. I really believed her!
   a. told someone something that wasn't true
   b. looked up something in the dictionary

4. Juliana is going to be a **participant** in a research study about teens and music.
   a. a person who takes part in an activity
   b. a person who leads scientific experiments

5. Many teenagers follow trends because they want their **peers** to like them.
   a. parents
   b. friends

6. The **researcher** wanted to find out how often radio stations play the most popular songs.
   a. someone who studies something
   b. someone who manages something

7. The **quality** of the food at the restaurant is excellent. It's expensive, but very delicious.
   a. how much of something there is
   b. how good or bad something is

8. The scientists did a **study** about the behavior of mice around different kinds of music.
   a. performance
   b. research project

PREVIEW READING 2

This is an article from a music magazine. The article discusses what makes a song become popular. It describes a research study that looks at how a song becomes popular.

What do you think the study will say? Check (✓) your answer.

- ☐ People make their music choices based on what other people like.
- ☐ People make their music choices based on what they like themselves.

CD 1
Track 4 **Read the magazine article.**

A Song Becomes a Hit

1   **W**hat makes a song become a popular **hit**? Do you think hit songs are popular because they are great songs? If so, you need to think again. **Researchers** say that hit songs become popular because listeners care about what other people think. For most listeners, the **quality** of the song is not as important.

2   A recent online **study** looked at how we choose our music. It showed that a song's popularity **influences** our choices. In other words, we like to listen to the music that our **peers** enjoy. In the study, researchers gave a list of 48 unknown songs to 14,000 teenagers. The students listened to some of the songs and rated them. **Participants** gave one star to songs that they didn't like. They gave five stars to songs that they liked very much.

3   The researchers divided the participants into two groups. The first group saw only the song title and the name of the band. They rated songs because the name of the song or the name of the

A recent study showed we like to listen to music our peers enjoy.

band looked interesting. After listening to the song, participants rated it with stars.

4   The second group of teenagers received extra information. This group could also see the number of downloads for each song. The songs with many downloads looked like they were very popular. The teenagers thought that these songs were favorites with their peers. However, the researchers **made up** the number of downloads for each song. The songs showing the most downloads weren't really popular. In fact, these songs weren't very good, according to music experts.

5   Participants in the second group usually gave the most stars to the songs with the most downloads. They thought these songs were popular with their peers. They were not interested in the quality of the song. They just wanted to listen to songs that their peers liked.

6   So why did participants give the most stars to the songs that seemed popular? One of the authors of the study, Matthew Salganik, a researcher at Columbia

University in New York, says: "People are faced with[1] too many options, in this case 48 songs. Since you can't listen to all of them, a natural shortcut[2] is to listen to what other people are listening to. I think that's what happens in the real world."

7   Salganik also says that people want to know what others are listening to. He says that people enjoy discussing and sharing music and books with their friends. So it isn't necessary for a popular book or a song to be of good quality. It is only necessary that some people enjoy it. Then these people influence their friends. And soon, the popularity of a song or book spreads. Perhaps it will even become a big hit.

8   Today the Internet lets people share their opinions about movies, books, and music almost instantly. People write about music on social networking sites, post comments on the Web, or read readers' reviews. On the Internet, a person can easily see how many people bought a book or downloaded a song. Perhaps this information has more influence on our choices than we think.

[1] **be faced with:** to have to deal with a situation
[2] **shortcut:** a quick or easy way to do something or get somewhere

MAIN IDEAS

Circle the correct answer to each question.

1. What is the main idea of the reading?
   a. Our peers influence our music choices.
   b. Some hit songs are not good songs.
   c. The researchers found that the two groups made different choices.

2. What is the main idea of paragraph 7?
   a. Most people are too lazy to make their own decisions.
   b. People often choose what to read or listen to because they want to share it with their friends.
   c. Quality is not important in our choices, especially with music and books.

DETAILS

Read the sentences. Then number them in the order that the information appears in Reading 2.

____ a.   The participants in the study were teenagers.

____ b.   The songs in the study were not known to the participants.

____ c.   There were two different groups in the study.

____ d.   The number of downloads was made up by the researchers.

____ e.   One group could see how many downloads each song had.

 **WHAT DO YOU THINK?**

A. Discuss the questions in a group.

1. How do you think the Internet can influence a song's popularity?

2. Do you think it's true that people choose to listen to the same music as their peers? Why or why not?

B. Think about both Reading 1 and Reading 2 as you discuss the questions. Then choose one question and write five to eight sentences in response.

1. Based on the readings, why do you think that something like a movie, song, or book becomes popular?

2. Imagine that you have created a new product. What would you do to try to make it become popular?

| Vocabulary Skill | Word families | |

Learning about **word families** can help you improve your vocabulary. Word families are groups of words that come from the same root. If you know the meaning of the *noun form* of a word, you may also recognize the *verb form*.

In some word families, the noun form and the verb form are the same.

His teacher had a strong **influence** on him.   Parents **influence** their children.
       └── noun   └── verb

In some word familes the noun form of the word is different from the verb form.

This **song** is popular.   I never **sing** in public.
     └── noun   └── verb

 **Tip for Success**

To help you determine if a word is a noun or a verb, remember that a noun is a person, place, or object, and a verb usually shows action.

A. Look at the pairs of words. Decide if each word is a noun or verb. Then write the words in the correct side of the chart on page 15. Use a dictionary to help you.

choice/choose	enjoy/enjoyment
connect/connection	gift/give
contribution/contribute	inform/information
discuss/discussion	think/thought

Nouns	Verbs
choice	*choose*

B. Read the sentences. Write *N* (noun) or *V* (verb) for each bold word.

_V_ 1. My brothers **study** in the kitchen every night.

___ 2. The **study** showed important changes in trends.

___ 3. Steven wanted to **comment** on Lilly's presentation.

___ 4. I saw the **comment** Penny wrote on the blog.

___ 5. The concert was a big **hit** with the students.

___ 6. Danilo's band **hit** it big with their new song.

___ 7. Dr. Lee's **research** is very important.

___ 8. Tom will **research** many colleges before making a decision.

___ 9. It is helpful to **preview** a reading before you begin.

___ 10. After I saw the movie **preview**, I didn't want to see the movie.

C. Complete each sentence with a noun or a verb from Activity B.

1. We often _____study_____ in the library at night.

2. Al usually likes to _____ a textbook chapter before he reads it.

3. The singer's first song was an instant _____ . Everyone loved it!

4. My parents always _____ on my clothing. They always have something to say about what I wear.

5. Carol will _____ new trends for her job at a magazine.

6. Allen wants to _____ sea animals at the university. He wants to be a marine biologist.

7. There is a new _____ about my photograph on my Web page every time I look. My site is really popular!

8. There's a _____ of the new movie on TV right now.

WRITING

When you write a paragraph, you need your main idea to be clear. One way to make sure your main idea is clear is to start your paragraph with a **topic sentence**. The topic sentence introduces the *topic* or subject of the paragraph. It also gives the *controlling idea*, which is what you want to say about the topic.

> topic   controlling idea
> Social networking sites are popular because people are social.
> Social networking sites are a waste of time.

Writing a topic sentence is an important part of making your writing clear.

A. Underline the topic sentence in this paragraph from Reading 2.

    A recent online study looked at how we choose our music. It showed that a song's popularity influences our choices. In other words, we like to listen to the music that our peers enjoy. In the study, researchers gave a list of 48 unknown songs to 14,000 teenagers. The students listened to some of the songs and rated them. Participants gave one star to songs that they didn't like. They gave five stars to songs that they liked very much.

B. Read the paragraphs. Choose the best topic sentence for each paragraph.

1. _____.
    They do this because it's fast and easy. In the time it takes to dial a number and say hello, you can send a text message. People also like to text instead of talking on the phone because it's silent. You can send messages from a meeting, but you can't make phone calls during a meeting. Text messaging is also convenient because you can send one message to several people at the same time. You can't do that with a phone call. For many reasons, text messaging has advantages over phone calls. Many people will continue to send text messages, until a new way of communicating comes along.

   a. Some people never make phone calls anymore.
   b. People use their cell phones only for text messages. They don't make phone calls.
   c. Many people today send text messages more often than they talk on the phone.

2.   Many students don't have computers at home. _____.
Students without computers can use the computers in their classrooms.
They can also learn important computer skills at school. If schools want
to provide the best education for students, they should make computers
available at school for their students. Studies show that students with good
computer skills have better chances of getting good jobs. Schools need
to provide computers for students whether or not they have computers
at home.

    a. All students should buy computers for their homes.
    b. Classroom computers are very helpful for students.
    c. Computer labs should be open all day.

3.   _____.
People of all ages are affected by this trend. Some people think that every
job will require people to use some kind of technology. Some people even
think that soon there will be computers that people actually wear as part
of their clothing. Others think that these ideas will never happen. But there
is no question that more and more, technology is a part of everyday life.

    a. It doesn't matter what your age is.
    b. Throughout the world, people are using more and more technology.
    c. Technology is getting smaller all the time.

C. **Read a student's paragraph. Then write a topic sentence for the
paragraph. Compare your topic sentence with a partner's.**

_____.

_____.

First of all, I usually don't like the new fashion trends. I have my own
fashion style. I usually buy well-made clothes, and I wear them for
many years. Some of my clothes are more than five years old. Buying
new clothes every year is very expensive. For example, trendy jeans
cost over $100. I buy clothes that I like, not the latest trends.

Use the **simple present** for habits and routines.

> I usually **buy** well-made clothes.
> I usually **check** my email every morning.

Use the **simple present** for factual information.

> Trendy jeans **cost** over $100.
> Over 5,000 teens **download** songs from that website.

Use the **simple present** for states and conditions.

> I **have** my own fashion style.
> I **know** a lot about computer games.

Use the **present continuous** for activities in progress or happening at the present moment.

> Eva **is checking** her email right now.
> **Are** you **downloading** music at home?

Use the **present continuous** for activities that are in progress, but not happening at the exact present moment.

> People **are checking** email on their phones these days.
> **Are** teenagers **buying** expensive jeans?

A. Read this paragraph from Reading 1. Underline verbs in the simple present. Compare your answers with a partner.

   Why is the social networking trend spreading so rapidly? One reason that these websites are popular is because people are social. We like to communicate with other people. We make friends with people in school, at work, and online. Most people like to stay closely connected to their friends and family. We use cell phones, email, instant messaging, and websites to learn what our friends are doing. The Internet is a good way to socialize and communicate, and social networking sites allow people to do this in many ways.

B. Complete each sentence with the simple present or present continuous form of the verb in parentheses.

1. Most high school students _____ (have) cell phones and the Internet.

2. Sue never _____ (write) letters to her friends anymore.

3. Gina _____ (watch) a popular TV show right now.

4. I _____ (use) the Internet for five hours every day.

5. Every summer Mari _____ (visit) her grandparents in Tokyo.

6. The radio station _____ (play) that hit song again. It's driving me crazy!

7. Every week, Erica _____ (take) more photos of her children.

8. Tom _____ (express) himself very well in his writing. I think he'll be an author some day.

9. Keiko _____ (plan) to study all day for the exam.

10. My brothers _____ (know) how to fix almost any kind of computer problem.

Unit Assignment | Write a descriptive paragraph

Q In this assignment, you will describe a trend that interests you and explain why it is popular. As you prepare your descriptive paragraph, think about the Unit Question, "Why does something become popular?" and refer to the Self-Assessment checklist on page 20.

For alternative unit assignments, see the *Q: Skills for Success Teacher's Handbook*.

PLAN AND WRITE

Tip for Success

When you brainstorm ideas before writing, think of as many ideas as you can. You don't need to use all of them. Just use the best ones.

A. BRAINSTORM Think about current trends. Write down as many ideas as you can. Brainstorm a list of as many trends as you can. For example, you can list trends in cars, music, food, or technology.

_____

_____

_____

B. PLAN Choose one trend from your list in A as your topic. Answer these questions. Then tell your partner about your topic.

1. What is the trend? Describe it.

_____

2. Does the trend help people connect with others? How?

_____

3. Why is the trend popular? What is new and different about it?

_____

4. How did this trend start and spread or become popular?

_____

Your Writing Process

For this activity you could also use Stage 1B, *Topic Sentence* in *Q Online Practice*.

C. **WRITE** Write a topic sentence for your paragraph. Include your topic and your controlling idea in your sentence. Then use some of your answers from Activity B to write your paragraph in your notebook. Look at the Self-Assessment checklist below to guide your writing.

REVISE AND EDIT

A. **PEER REVIEW** Read your partner's paragraph. Answer the questions and discuss them with your partner.

1. Is there a topic sentence? Can you identify the topic and the controlling idea?

2. Is there a clear description of the trend?

3. Is there one idea that is very strong? Put a star (★) in the margin next to it.

4. Write one or two questions about your partner's topic.

B. **REWRITE** Review the answers from Activity A. You may want to revise and rewrite your paragraph.

 **for Success**

Read your paragraph more than once. For example, read once only for verb tenses and read again only for punctuation errors.

C. **EDIT** Complete the Self-Assessment checklist as you prepare to write the final draft of your paragraph. Be prepared to hand in your work or discuss it in class.

SELF-ASSESSMENT		
Yes	No	
☐	☐	Is the first line of the paragraph indented?
☐	☐	Does each sentence start with a capital letter and end with a period or question mark?
☐	☐	Is each word spelled correctly? Check a dictionary if you are not sure.
☐	☐	Is there vocabulary from the unit in the paragraph?
☐	☐	Underline all of the verbs in the simple present and present continuous. Are they in the correct form?

Track Your Success

Circle the words you learned in this unit.

Nouns	Verbs	Phrasal Verbs
hit 🔑	contribute 🔑 AWL	find out 🔑
participant AWL	express 🔑	make up 🔑
peer	influence 🔑	**Phrases**
researcher AWL	spread 🔑	connected to
study 🔑	**Adjective**	keep in touch
trend 🔑 AWL	clear 🔑	
quality 🔑		

🔑 Oxford 3000™ words

AWL Academic Word List

For more information on the Oxford 3000™ and the AWL, see page xi.

Check (✓) the skills you learned. If you need more work on a skill, refer to the page(s) in parentheses.

READING ⚪	I can identify the main idea of a paragraph. (p. 9)
VOCABULARY ⚪	I can use noun and verb forms in word families. (p. 14)
WRITING ⚪	I can write a topic sentence. (p. 16)
GRAMMAR ⚪	I can use the simple present and the present continuous. (p. 18)
LEARNING OUTCOME ⚪	I can write a paragraph describing a current trend and why it is popular.

Unit QUESTION

How do colors affect the way we feel?

PREVIEW THE UNIT

A Discuss these questions with your classmates.

What's your favorite color? Why do you like it?

Imagine that you walk into a room that has yellow walls. How does that color make you feel?

Look at the photo. How do the colors in the room make you feel?

B Discuss the Unit Question above with your classmates.

Listen to *The Q Classroom*, Track 5 on CD 1, to hear other answers.

C Look at the pictures and read the captions. Then discuss the questions.

1. What color is special for each person? Why?

2. Valeria McCullock likes the color blue. It makes her feel peaceful. She says that for her wearing blue is being in a dream all day. How does the color blue make you feel?

3. What colors do you like to wear? Why?

4. What colors do you not like to wear? Why?

1

Valeria McCullock wears only blue. She says blue makes her feel peaceful. "Wearing blue for me is being in a dream all day," she says.

2

Tom Le's favorite color is red. He says, "I like red because it's a warm, bright color. Red makes me feel happy."

3

All of Stephin Merritt's clothes are brown. It's easy to wear brown, he says, because all browns go together. Also, brown doesn't show dirt or stains. Merritt says, "I have brown hair and eyes, and I believe in matching."

4

Elizabeth Sweetheart dresses in green. It makes her think of nature—trees, flowers, grass. "I missed nature when I moved to New York," she says.

READING 1 | How Colors Make Us Think and Feel

VOCABULARY

Here are some words from Reading 1. Read the sentences. Then write each bold word next to the correct definition.

1. The weather can **affect** us. When it's cold and rainy, many people feel sad.

2. When Alex came to Miami from Russia, it was hard for him to understand some things about American **culture**. For example, he didn't understand why people wore jeans to nice restaurants.

3. You often know what **emotion** a person is feeling even if they don't say anything. People cry when they are sad, and smile or laugh when they are happy.

4. After Ana lost her job, she started having **psychological** problems. It was very stressful for her, so she worried a lot and felt very sad.

5. Jim's doctor told him to do some **specific** things to improve his health. He told him to exercise twice a week and eat less junk food.

6. The color red has many meanings. It can **represent** love, anger, or "stop."

7. Tom is **unaware** of how loudly he talks on his cell phone, so he keeps doing it.

8. It's a **universal** belief that friendship is important. I don't know anyone who doesn't think so.

a. _____ (*n.*) the way of doing things, ideas, and beliefs of a particular society

b. _____ (*adj.*) connected with or true for everyone in the world or in a particular group

c. _____ (*adj.*) not knowing or noticing someone or something

d. _____ (*v.*) to be a picture, example, or sign of something

e. _____ (*v.*) to make someone or something change in a particular way, to influence someone or something

f. _____ (*adj.*) connected with the mind or the way it works

g. _____ (*n.*) a strong feeling, such as fear or anger

h. _____ (*adj.*) particular, not general

Tip for Success

Before you read, preview a text to get a general idea of the content. Read the title and look at any pictures and captions. If there are section titles, read them.

PREVIEW READING 1

This is an article from a psychology textbook that discusses colors and cultural differences. It shows some of the ways color can affect people.

Preview the article by looking at the titles and photos. Which section do you think will discuss different countries?

_____

 CD 1 Track 6   **Read the textbook article.**

How Colors Make Us Think and Feel

What does the color pink make you think of? How does the color blue make you feel? Why do hospital doctors wear white coats? What color room makes you feel relaxed?

Colors affect everyone

1   Each person may have a different answer to these questions, but we can agree that colors **affect** everyone. We think carefully about color when we choose our clothes or select paint for a room. But we are often **unaware** of how color affects us. For example, the color of a room may affect our **emotions**. Advertisers use color to influence our choices at the supermarket. In addition, we may not realize that colors have many different meanings.

Universal meaning

2   Colors in nature have **universal** meaning. For example, trees and plants are green, so the color green often **represents** life and nature. Blue, the color of the sky, oceans, and lakes, makes us think of air, water, and peace. Colors in the red spectrum[1]—yellow, orange, and red—are warm colors. Those colors may give us a feeling of warmth and comfort or feelings of anger. Colors in the blue spectrum—colors such as blue, green, and purple—are cool colors. They often give a feeling of calmness or sadness. These ideas about color are similar around the world.

Colors in health

3   Humans have known about the power of color for a long time. Ancient **cultures** in China, Egypt, and India used colors to heal sicknesses. People believed that each

A Color Wheel

[1] **spectrum:** a group of colors

color had a healing power. For example, people used blue to decrease pain. Even today, some people say that colors can help people feel better. However, research shows that although colors may change the way a person feels, they cannot heal an illness.

Cultural meaning

4   Colors also have different meanings in different cultures. A color may represent good feelings in one culture but bad feelings in another. For example, in the United States, white represents goodness. It is usually the color of a bride's wedding dress. However, in India, China, and Japan, white can mean death. Green is the color of dollar bills in the U.S., so green may make Americans think of money. But in China, green can represent a loss of respect[2]. Different colors sometimes represent the same idea in different cultures. In European cultures, purple is the color of royalty for kings and queens. In Asia, yellow is the color of royalty. In addition, one color will have many different meanings within one culture. For example, in North America, red often means stop or danger, but it also can represent love.

Color psychology

5   Color **psychology** is the study of how colors affect our emotions. Researchers are finding that colors can change our behavior in **specific** ways. For example, one research study showed

The bride and groom at a Korean wedding

that people could lift heavy weights more easily in blue rooms. Other studies have looked at how colors influence decisions. Soccer referees made more decisions against teams that wore black uniforms. Tae kwon do[3] referees gave competitors in blue clothing higher scores than competitors in red. In another study, students who saw the color red before a test did much more poorly. Of course, these test results might vary from culture to culture.

6   Most people do not realize how much color affects them. It can affect how people think, feel, and act. Some colors, such as those in nature, can have the same meaning for everyone. Other color meanings may be different in different cultures. We can increase our understanding of ourselves and the world around us by learning about what colors can mean or represent.

[2] **respect:** the feeling that someone or something is important

[3] **tae kwon do:** a Korean art of self-defense using kicks

MAIN IDEAS

Read the statements. Write *T* (true) or *F* (false).

_____ 1. Most of us are unaware of how colors affect us.

_____ 2. A color only has one meaning.

_____ 3. For people around the world, colors in nature have similar meanings.

_____ 4. Some people believed that colors could heal people.

_____ 5. Research studies about color psychology show that color does not affect our actions or emotions.

DETAILS

A. Look at the colors listed in the chart below. Some examples are done for you. Write what each color represents. Look at the article to check your answers.

Blue	Green	Red	Yellow	White
air	go	stop	warmth	goodness

 WHAT DO YOU THINK?

Discuss the questions in a group. Then choose one question and write five to eight sentences in response.

1. According to the article, soccer referees made more decisions against teams wearing black uniforms. Why do you think that happened?

2. What are some examples of colors with special meanings in your culture? You may want to think about colors used for special occasions such as weddings, birthdays, funerals, or holidays.

3. Think about the color of your bedroom or living room. How does the color make you feel? Would you like to change the color? Why or why not?

Reading Skill | Getting meaning from context

If you find a word you don't know in a text, you can use the **context** to help you understand the meaning of the word. The context is the other words near the unknown word. Looking up every new word in the dictionary will slow your reading. Instead, use the context to help you understand the general meaning of a word.

context

It was a **joyful** celebration. Everyone was very happy.

context

The red sign told me that there was **danger** and some possibility of injury.

From the context, you can understand that the word **joyful** means *very happy*. From the example, you can understand that **danger** means *a chance that someone might get hurt.*

Tip Critical Thinking

In Activities A and B, you have to **use** the context to understand the meaning of new words. **Using** context to guess meaning can help you read more fluently.

A. Read these sentences from Reading 1. Underline the words that give the context for the bold word in each sentence.

1. Those colors may give us a **feeling** of <u>warmth</u> and <u>comfort</u> or feelings of <u>anger</u>.

2. Ancient cultures in China, Egypt, and India used colors to **heal** sicknesses. For example, people used blue to decrease pain.

3. In the United States, white usually represents goodness. It is usually the color of a **bride's** wedding dress.

4. In European cultures, purple is the color of **royalty** for kings and queens.

5. Color **psychology** is the study of how colors affect your emotions.

6. Soccer **referees** made more decisions against teams that wore black uniforms.

B. Write a definition for each word from Activity A. Then check your definitions in your dictionary.

1. feeling _____

2. heal _____

3. bride _____

4. royalty _____

5. psychology _____

6. referees _____

READING 2 | The Importance of Color in Business

VOCABULARY

Here are some words from Reading 2. Read the sentences. Circle the answer that best matches the meaning of each bold word.

1. **Advertising** in newspapers and on the radio helped the restaurant increase its business.
   a. writing articles
   b. telling people about products
   c. talking to customers

2. Choosing a college is difficult. I have to carefully **consider** all my choices.
   a. think about
   b. be worried about
   c. measure

3. My car is not very **dependable**. My battery died three times this month!
   a. important
   b. forceful
   c. reliable

4. I'm going to **encourage** Jorge to apply for the new job at the radio station. I think it's the perfect job for him.
   a. convince
   b. research
   c. command

5. Our family recycles paper and plastic to help protect the **environment**.
   a. machines
   b. natural world
   c. people

6. She left her job at the advertising company and wants to **establish** her own company.
   a. create
   b. sell
   c. research

7. A **service** that many hotels offer is helping with luggage.
   a. relationship between companies
   b. thing that a company does for you
   c. rule that a company follows

8. These new cell phones come in a **variety** of colors. I don't know which one to choose!
   a. large selection
   b. small choice
   c. very tiny group

PREVIEW READING 2

This is an article from a business magazine. The article talks about color psychology and describes how colors can affect the way people think about specific companies. Preview the article and circle the names of seven companies. What do you already know about these companies?

 CD 1
Track 7 **Read the magazine article.**

The Importance of Color in Business

1   If you walk into a McDonald's restaurant, what colors will you see? Probably yellow and red. And when you think about McDonald's, you will think about those two bright and cheerful colors. Every year large companies spend millions of dollars on **advertising**. They want you to buy their products and use their **services**, and they want you to remember their company name. Companies use color so that you will notice them and so that you will think about them when you see their colors. One research project showed that color helps people remember company names. Colors are very important to businesses.

2   Blue is often used by computer companies. IBM, Microsoft and Dell all use the color blue to show that their companies are serious and **dependable**. Like the sky and the ocean, blue can be both peaceful and powerful. To show that their computers are for serious people, many companies used to make their computers black or gray. But Apple computer company decided that they wanted computers to be fun instead of serious. For that reason, they made their iMac computers in a variety of different colors in the late 1990s. Today, their iPods come in a **variety** of colors.

3   BP uses green and yellow for its colors. It is the only large oil company to use green. Green is the color of nature. Yellow is the color of the sun. Both colors are bright and cheerful. BP hopes that people will think of it as a friendly company. In addition, green may make you think of the **environment**. BP wants people to think of it as a company that cares about the environment.

4   United Parcel Service (UPS) is a big delivery company. Its company color is brown. When UPS started in the 1920s, brown was a good color for a safe, reliable company. From the beginning, UPS used brown trucks and brown uniforms. In today's world,

A UPS delivery man

brown may seem like a boring color choice for a company. But UPS decided to make it a positive symbol of its business. Their ads ask, "What can brown do for you?" When people see the big brown UPS trucks, the company hopes they will think of excellent, dependable service.

5   All over the world, companies use color to **establish** their brand[1] and to encourage people to buy their products. Companies believe that customers respond strongly to their colors. It isn't surprising that companies carefully **consider** the colors for their products and their advertising.

[1] **brand:** the name of a product that is made by a specific company

MAIN IDEAS

Check (✓) the main idea of the article.

____ 1.   Companies don't care if you remember their colors, as long as you buy their products.

____ 2.   Companies use color so you will notice them and remember their company when you see their colors.

____ 3.   Blue is a good color for computer companies.

____ 4.   Many companies use green because it shows they care about the environment.

DETAILS

A. Complete the chart with information from the article.

Name of company	Company colors	Feelings that colors give
McDonald's	red and yellow	bright, cheerful
		dependable, peaceful, powerful
	variety of colors	
BP		
	brown	

B. Write one or two sentences to describe each company, their colors, and the meaning of the colors. Use your answers from Activity A.

1. McDonald's: <u>McDonald's uses red and yellow because they are bright and</u>

    <u>cheerful colors</u>

2. UPS: _____

3. computer companies: _____

4. BP: _____

 # WHAT DO YOU THINK?

A. Discuss these questions in a group.

1. Choose three companies from Reading 2. Then note the color or colors that each company uses. Do you think that the colors they use influence how you think of them? Why or why not?

2. Imagine that you are designing a new restaurant. Decide what kind of restaurant it is. Then choose colors for the restaurant, the signs, the walls, the plates, the napkins. What colors would you use? Why?

B. Think about both Reading 1 and Reading 2 as you discuss the questions. Then choose one question and write five to eight sentences in response.

1. Think of a company or service that you are familiar with. What colors does it use for its products and advertising? Do you think the company is using color psychology? How?

2. Imagine that you are going to design a library for children. What colors would you use for the tables and shelves, for the walls, and for a reading area? Why would you use those colors?

A **suffix** is a letter or group of letters at the end of a word. A suffix changes the form of a word. Common suffixes for changing a noun to an adjective are *–ful* and *–al*.

Nathaniel's favorite **color** is purple.
noun

Elizabeth loved to draw **colorful** pictures.
adjective

The researcher finished the **experiment** in one month.
noun

The tests were **experimental**, and they didn't prove anything.
adjective

Understanding suffixes can help you increase your vocabulary. If you know the meaning of a noun, then you may be able to also understand its adjective form.

Noun	Adjective
cheer	cheerful
joy	joyful
education	educational
nation	national

Sometimes when you add a suffix, there are spelling changes to the noun form.

Noun	Adjective
biology	biological
finance	financial

A. Read each sentence. Write *N* (noun) or *ADJ* (adjective) for each bold word.

_N_ 1   Martin left his restaurant in his son's **care**.

____ 2.   Laura was **careful** when she chose a company logo.

____ 3.   The color green is a **universal** symbol of nature.

____ 4.   Kathryn feels small when she thinks about how big the **universe** is.

____ 5.   **Psychology** was Mary's favorite subject in college.

____ 6.   The doctor was concerned about Alan's **psychological** problems.

____ 7.   The president greeted the king with a **respectful** bow.

____ 8.   The new police officer quickly won the **respect** of the local residents.

B. Complete the chart with the correct form of each word. Then check your answers in the dictionary.

Nouns	Adjectives
1. addition	additional
2. culture	
3. emotion	
4. environment	
5. nature	
6.	peaceful
7.	personal
8. power	

Tip for Success

When you learn a new word, look in the dictionary for its other forms such as noun, verb, adjective, and adverb. This is an easy way to expand your vocabulary.

C. Complete the paragraph with a noun or adjective from Activity B.

Many people don't like running because they think it's difficult, but I really enjoy it. I usually run in a beautiful, big park near my house. There are lots of trees, flowers, and birds in the park. I like running there because I like _____. The park is far away
1
from the noise and stress of the city, so it's very quiet and _____. Some people prefer to run
2
with another _____, but I prefer to
3
run alone, especially before work. My job is very stressful, but running helps me feel more relaxed. I think it's good for my physical and

_____ health. I usually run three miles every morning, but
4
sometimes I have time for a(n) _____ mile or two. Maybe
5
someday I'll run ten miles!

WRITING

Freewriting is a good way to brainstorm ideas before you write. In freewriting, you write down all of your thoughts about a topic or a question. Freewriting is a good strategy for many kinds of problem-solving, whether at work, in another class, or at home. It helps you think freely and creatively. Here are some tips for freewriting.

- Write down every idea that comes to you for five or ten minutes.
- Don't worry about whether an idea is a good one or not.
- Try to stay focused and write only about your topic.
- Look at your ideas. Choose the best ideas to develop for your writing.

A. Read the freewriting example about the topic below. Cross out the information that does not focus on the topic. Then compare your answers with a partner.

> **Topic:** How do companies use color to advertise their products? Write about companies that use color effectively.
>
> Companies and colors, Internet companies—Google uses lots of different colors, they are bright, happy colors—e-Bay also uses many different bright colors. Are they the same colors? My brother bought a bicycle on e-Bay. He rides it to work. Stores—Macy's department store uses red. I like the color red. It's a strong, exciting color. Macy's uses a red star in its advertisements. I always think of the red star and Macy's. Sometimes I shop at Macy's. The red star is a good symbol. It's easy to remember and recognize.

B. Here's the beginning of a paragraph about the topic from Activity A. Underline the information in Activity A that can be used in the paragraph.

Macy's and Target, two large department stores, both use the color red in their advertising.

C. Read the questions below. Then follow the steps to brainstorm and share your ideas.

Topic: Think of a well-known restaurant, clothing store, department store, or a company such as an airline. How does the company use color in their advertising or inside their place of business? How do the colors make you feel?

Steps

1. Freewrite about the questions. First, choose a business to write about. Then freewrite for five to ten minutes. Write down all of your ideas. Don't worry about grammar or spelling right now.

2. After you stop writing, read through your notes. Underline the ideas you want to use in your writing.

3. Share your freewriting with your partner. Explain your ideas and answer any questions.

D. Write a paragraph about the topic in your notebook. Use your freewriting from Activity C and any new ideas.

Grammar | Conjunctions

Conjunctions are words that join other words, phrases, or sentences. The words *and*, *but*, *or*, and *so* are conjunctions.

Use *and* to add information to a sentence, or to join two sentences that are similar. Put a comma before *and* when it joins two sentences.

> It was cold **and** windy today.
> I called Yumiko, **and** she told me what happened.

Use *or* when combining ideas or sentences when there is a choice or more than one possibility. Put a comma before *or* when it joins two sentences.

> Do you want ice cream **or** cake for dessert?
> We could take the train to Madrid, **or** we could drive.

Use *but* to join two contrasting ideas or sentences. Put a comma before *but* when it joins two sentences.

> It's sunny **but** cold today.
> Monica liked the book, **but** she didn't like the movie.

Use *so* to show a result. Put a comma before *so*.

> It was raining, **so** we didn't go to the beach.
> The bus was late, **so** I walked.

A. Read the sentences. Then add commas where necessary. The first one is done for you.

1. Paul looked all over the house for his glasses, but he didn't find them.

2. It's very hot and sunny in Miami today.

3. I saw Maria today and she looked very upset.

4. The children are tired and hungry.

5. Felix was sick so he didn't go to work.

6. You can take the subway or the bus.

7. Sandra has a brother but she doesn't have any sisters.

8. You can take the test today or you can take it on Monday.

B. Complete each sentence with the correct conjunction. Use commas correctly.

1. My brother is usually dependable __, but__ last night he forgot to pick me up after class.

2. That department store has a good selection of clothing _____ I shop there often.

3. I think many TV advertisements are stupid _____ annoying.

4. We could go out for dinner _____ we could eat at home.

5. Ali went to his sister's house yesterday _____ she made lunch for him.

6. I can ski _____ I can't skate.

7. Jason didn't study _____ he failed the test.

8. It's going to be warm _____ sunny on Saturday. Let's go hiking!

9. My computer wasn't working yesterday _____ I didn't get your email until this morning.

10. Do you prefer bright colors like red and yellow _____ dark colors like blue and gray?

11. Paul looked all over the house for his glasses _____ he couldn't find them.

12. Tanya has three sisters _____ one brother.

In this assignment you will write a description of a new business you create. Your description will include information about what colors you will use and why. As you prepare to write, think about the Unit Question, "How do colors affect the way we feel?" and refer to the Self-Assessment checklist on page 40.

For alternative unit assignments, see the *Q: Skills for Success Teacher's Handbook.*

PLAN AND WRITE

Your Writing Process

For this activity you could also use Stage 1A, *Clustering*, in *Q Online Practice.*

A. **BRAINSTORM** Choose a business. Your new business could sell a product such as clothing, computers, or a type of food. Or your business could be a service such as a restaurant, repair shop, school, airline, or health service.

B. **PLAN** Freewrite ideas about your new business in your notebook.

1. Freewrite ideas for your new business in your notebook. Think about these questions as you freewrite.
   - What kind of business is it?
   - What is the name of your business?
   - What colors do you want to use for the inside of your business and your advertisements?
   - Why do you want to use these colors?
   - How do you want these colors to make your customers feel?

2. Discuss your ideas from your freewriting with a partner. Answer any questions your partner has about your ideas. Decide which ideas are the best. Underline your best ideas.

C. **WRITE** Use your notes from Activity B to complete your color proposal. Fill out the top part of the form. Then write a paragraph to explain your plan in your notebook. Use compound sentences. Look at the Self-Assessment checklist on page 40 to guide your writing.

New Business Proposal

Company name: _____

Product or service: _____

Main colors (two or three): _____

Reason for choosing these colors:

_____

_____

REVISE AND EDIT

A. **PEER REVIEW** Read your partner's color proposal. Answer the questions and discuss them with your partner.

1. Is the purpose of the business clear?

2. Do you think that the business will be popular? Explain.

3. Is there a clear explanation for the colors the business will use?

4. Put a star (★) in the margin next to the best ideas in the proposal.

5. Write one or two questions that you have about the proposal.

B. **REWRITE** Review the answers to the questions in Activity A. You may want to revise and rewrite your proposal.

C. **EDIT** Complete the Self-Assessment checklist as you prepare to write the final draft of your proposal. Be prepared to hand in your work or discuss it in class.

Yes	No	SELF-ASSESSMENT
☐	☐	Does each sentence start with a capital letter and end with a period or question mark?
☐	☐	Is each word spelled correctly? Check a dictionary if you are not sure.
☐	☐	Is there vocabulary from the unit in the proposal?
☐	☐	Do you use any adjectives with suffixes? Did you use the correct suffixes?
☐	☐	Do you use conjunctions and commas correctly?

Circle the words you learned in this unit.

Nouns
advertising 🔑
bride
culture 🔑 AWL
danger 🔑
emotion 🔑
environment 🔑 AWL
feeling 🔑
psychology AWL
referee
royalty

service 🔑
variety 🔑

Verbs
affect 🔑 AWL
consider 🔑
encourage 🔑
establish 🔑 AWL
heal 🔑
represent 🔑

Adjectives
dependable
joyful
psychological AWL
specific 🔑 AWL
unaware AWL
universal 🔑

🔑 Oxford 3000™ words
AWL Academic Word List

Check (✓) the skills you learned. If you need more work on a skill, refer to the pages in parentheses.

READING	●	I can get meaning from context. (p. 29)
VOCABULARY	●	I can use suffixes to change word forms. (p. 34)
WRITING	●	I can freewrite. (p. 36)
GRAMMAR	●	I can use conjunctions correctly in sentences. (p. 37)
LEARNING OUTCOME	●	I can write a description of a new business that explains the colors I will use and why.

READING ●	identifying supporting details
VOCABULARY ●	prefixes
WRITING ●	supporting your main idea with examples
GRAMMAR ●	subject-verb agreement

Write a paragraph in response to a question on an online discussion forum about politeness.

Unit QUESTION

What does it mean to be polite?

PREVIEW THE UNIT

A Discuss these questions with your classmates.

Describe a time when someone was rude to you. What happened? What did you do?

Who taught you how to be polite?

Look at the photo. What are the people doing? Why?

B Discuss the Unit Question above with your classmates.

Listen to *The Q Classroom*, Track 8 on CD 1, to hear other answers.

C How polite do you think you should be to these people? Check (✓) your answers.

	A little polite		Polite		Very polite
	1	2	3	4	5
police officer	☐	☐	☐	☐	☑
teacher	☐	☐	☐	☐	☐
classmate	☐	☐	☐	☐	☐
brother/sister	☐	☐	☐	☐	☐
parent	☐	☐	☐	☐	☐
young child	☐	☐	☐	☐	☐
store manager	☐	☐	☐	☐	☐
sales person	☐	☐	☐	☐	☐
boss	☐	☐	☐	☐	☐
co-worker	☐	☐	☐	☐	☐

D Think about things a parent in your culture would teach a child about being polite or rude. Write your answers in the T-chart below. Then compare them with a partner's.

Polite	Rude
saying "please" and "thank you"	talking loudly in public

READING 1 | **Being Polite from Culture to Culture**

VOCABULARY

Here are some words from Reading 1. Read the sentences. Then write each bold word next to the correct definition.

1. I had an **awkward** conversation with my friend about money. He always borrows money and forgets to repay me.

2. Sam has really bad **manners**. He never says "please" or "thank you" to anyone, and he often talks with food in his mouth.

3. My nephews dressed **appropriately** for the wedding. They wore nice, clean suits.

4. Psychologists are interested in human **behavior**. They are studying what people do in different situations.

5. When the president entered the room, everyone stood up as a sign of **respect**.

6. Nat held his daughter's hand **firmly** when they crossed the street. He wanted to make sure she walked next to him.

7. When you have a job interview, it's important to **make a good impression**. You should dress well, arrive on time, and ask questions.

8. Laura made a **gesture** to ask the waiter to bring the check because she didn't want to shout across the restaurant.

a. _____ (n.) polite behavior toward someone or something you think is important

b. _____ (n.) the way you act or behave

c. _____ (adj.) not comfortable, embarrassing

d. _____ (v.) to produce a good effect or opinion

e. _____ (adv.) in a strong, steady way

f. _____ (n.) the way of acting that is considered polite in your society or culture

g. _____ (adv.) suitable or right for a particular situation

h. _____ (n.) a movement of the hand or head to express something

PREVIEW READING 1

This is an article from a travel magazine that talks about politeness in different cultures. It gives examples from North America, the Middle East, Latin America, and Asia.

What are some things you think might be considered polite in some cultures, but not in others?

_____

_____

 CD 1
Track 9   **Read the magazine article.**

Being Polite from Culture to Culture

1   Most people want to be polite and behave well around others. Being polite means knowing how to greet and talk to people. It means using good **manners** when eating. It means knowing how to give and receive gifts **appropriately**. Polite **behavior** in one country, however, may be impolite in another part of the world. Travelers need to understand the cultural differences in politeness so that they don't cause embarrassment.

2   For instance, when people meet, they often shake hands. How long should a handshake be? Should you hold the other person's hand gently or **firmly**? In the United States, people prefer to shake hands firmly for a few seconds. In some Middle Eastern countries, people hold the person's hand gently for a longer time. Handshaking varies around the world.

3   What about eye contact[1]? In some countries you show **respect** when you look someone directly in the eye. In other parts of the world,

to look at someone directly is rude. To be respectful, a person looks down at the ground.

4   There are also cultural differences in the way people use personal space[2]. When two people are talking, should they stand close together or far apart? Exactly how close should they stand? In North America, for instance, people usually stand about an arm's length

In some countries making eye contact shows respect.

---

[1] **eye contact:** a look directly into someone else's eyes   [2] **personal space:** the area that is close to a person

apart during a conversation. However, in some countries in the Middle East and Latin America, people stand closer. It can be **awkward** if one person likes to stand close and the other person likes to stand farther apart.

5   Three authors wrote a book *Kiss, Bow, or Shake Hands* about cultural differences. In their book, they discuss greetings, gift-giving, and time. Around the world cultures have different ideas about giving gifts. In the United States,

Being polite means knowing how to give and receive gifts appropriately.

if someone gives you a gift, you should open it while they are with you. That way they can see how happy you are to receive it. In China, you should open a gift after the person is gone.

6   Another cultural difference is time. If someone invites you to dinner at their house at 6 p.m., what time should you get there? Should you arrive early, late, or exactly on time? In Germany, it is important to arrive on time. In Argentina, polite dinner guests usually come 30 to 60 minutes after the time of the invitation. When traveling, remember that each country has a different definition of being on time.

7   A final area to be careful about is body language, including **gestures**. Is it acceptable to touch a person on the shoulder? How do you wave goodbye or hello? How do you gesture to someone to "come here"? All of these can be different from one culture to another. In Thailand, it is rude to touch someone on the head with the palm of the hand. The gesture for "come here" in the U.S. is only used for calling animals in some other countries.

8   If you are going to live, work, or study in another country, it is important to learn the language. But it is also important to learn about cultural differences. This way, you can be polite and **make a good impression**. People around you will feel comfortable and respected. Politeness and good manners can be good for making friends, good for traveling, and good for business, too.

MAIN IDEAS

Read the statements. Write *T* (true) or *F* (false).

____ 1.   Polite behavior is the same everywhere.

____ 2.   People make eye contact in different ways in different cultures.

____ 3.   Most people are comfortable with same amount of personal space.

____ 4.   Being on time is important in every culture.

____ 5.   Some gestures are polite in one country and rude in another.

____ 6.   It's only important to know what is polite in your own country.

DETAILS

Circle the answer to each question.

1. How do people in the United States prefer to shake hands?
   a. firmly for a short time
   b. gently for a short time
   c. firmly for a long time

2. How closely do people in Latin America or the Middle East like to stand while talking?
   a. at an arm's length
   b. more than an arm's length
   c. more closely than an arm's length

3. What should you do if someone in China gives you a gift?
   a. open it in front of the person
   b. wait until the person has left before opening it
   c. open the gift immediately

4. You are invited for dinner at 7:00 p.m. in Germany. What time should you arrive?
   a. 6:45 p.m.
   b. 7:00 p.m.
   c. 7:30 p.m.

5. If you show that you understand cultural differences and politeness, how will people feel?
   a. comfortable and respected
   b. uncomfortable and awkward
   c. polite and happy

 WHAT DO YOU THINK?

Discuss the questions in a group. Then choose one question and write five to eight sentences in response.

1. In your culture, what is the polite way to greet someone, to receive a gift, and to say goodbye to a friend?

2. How can being polite help you at school or at work? Give specific examples.

A well-written article includes **details** that support the main ideas. Details can be facts, reasons, or examples. Identifying **supporting details** will help you understand the main ideas of an article.

Main Idea ⌐ Bowing is a form of greeting in many countries.

Supporting Details ⌐

fact: something you know is true

Bowing is the traditional greeting in East Asia.

reason: the cause of something

People bow low when greeting older people because it is a sign of respect.

example: something that shows what something is like

In a very formal bow, the forehead sometimes touches the floor.

Identifying and underlining important supporting details as you read can help you improve your reading comprehension.

A. Reread paragraph 4 in Reading 1. Look at the main idea of the paragraph. Write two details that support it. Then compare your answers with a partner.

_____

_____

B. Reread paragraph 5. Answer these questions. Then compare your answers with a partner.

1. What is the main idea? _____

2. How many supporting details are in the paragraph? What are they?

_____

C. Reread paragraph 6. Answer these questions. Then compare your answers with a partner.

1. What is the main idea? _____

2. What examples does the writer use as supporting details?

_____

READING 2 | Answers to All Your Travel Questions!

VOCABULARY

Here are some words from Reading 2. Read the sentences. Circle the answer that best matches the meaning of each bold word or phrase.

1. My uncle gave me some good **advice** about starting a business.
   a. money that someone loans you
   b. proverb or famous quote
   c. words that help someone decide what to do

2. A **custom** you will notice when you go to Japan is that people don't wear their shoes inside their homes.
   a. way of life
   b. thing for sale
   c. party

3. Classes at many universities are **informal**. Students can bring food to class and ask questions whenever they want.
   a. lengthy; taking a long time
   b. relaxed and friendly
   c. useful and informative

4. It's rude to **interrupt** someone when they are speaking. You should always let them finish.
   a. make someone stop talking
   b. repeat over and over
   c. whisper; talk quietly

5. I want to **take part in** the meeting about the neighborhood school. I think it's going to be very interesting.
   a. divide up; separate
   b. join, participate in
   c. act in

6. It's **traditional** in some countries for the bride to wear a white dress for the wedding. In other countries the bride wears red.
   a. inexpensive
   b. doing what others want you to do
   c. ways of doing things that have existed for a long time

7. Try to **avoid** talking when you have food in your mouth. It's very rude!
   a. choose not to do
   b. adjust
   c. continue

8. On a **typical** day, Erik works from 9:00 a.m. to 5:00 p.m., but today he worked until 7:30 p.m.

a. pleasant

b. awkward

c. usual

Tip for Success

In online posts, people often use informal language. For example, they may shorten a sentence so it doesn't follow the typical rules of grammar.

PREVIEW READING 2

This is an online discussion group where people can post comments about a topic. In the forum travelers ask for advice about customs in different countries.

What kinds of topics do you think the travelers will ask about?

☐ greeting people   ☐ giving/receiving gifts

☐ conversation topics   ☐ table manners

☐ other _____

 CD 1 Track 10   **Read the posts from the travel forum.**

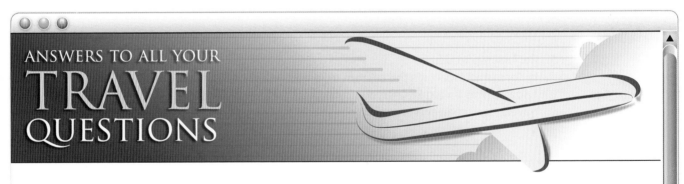

ANSWERS TO ALL YOUR
TRAVEL
QUESTIONS

Yong Jun Park, Seoul
Posted: 3 days ago

Question: First trip to U.S.
For my new job, I will travel to the United States next month and meet my American boss. This will be my first trip to the U.S. I'm worried about correct business etiquette[1] and manners. My boss invited me to his home for dinner. Do you have any **advice**?
REPLY

Sue, Miami
Posted: 3 days ago

1. **Re:** First trip to U.S.
It's a good idea to bring a small gift or something from your country. Don't be surprised if your boss opens the gift right away. In the U.S., people often open a gift when they receive it. In Korea, that is not polite, but it's appropriate in the U.S.
REPLY

[1] **etiquette:** polite and correct behavior in a social situation

2. Re: First trip to U.S.
Many Americans are very **informal** at home. One time I went to dinner at the home of an American business partner. I was surprised that everyone stood and talked in the kitchen while the husband and wife cooked dinner. Also, unlike in Korea, everyone **took part in** the dinner table conversation, even the man's wife and children.
REPLY

Jun, Seoul
Posted:
2 days ago

3. Re: First trip to U.S.
I agree with Jun. I was surprised that American men often cook and that both the husband and wife come to the dinner table and talk. You probably won't speak about business during dinner, so my advice is to know some good topics of conversation. For example, you can talk about travel, food, music, or sports. Of course, it's good to ask about your boss's family. But it's not polite to ask questions about age, salary, religion, or politics.
REPLY

Andrea,
Santiago
Posted:
12 hours ago

4. Re: First trip to U.S.
Americans use their hands to eat some kinds of food, such as pizza and fried chicken. Watch your American hosts², and do what they do.
REPLY

Sun Hee Choi,
Pusan
Posted:
8 hours ago

5. Re: First trip to U.S.
In Korea and Japan, it's the **custom** to remove your shoes before entering a house. In the United States, you usually don't take your shoes off. Once I was traveling in Japan and entered a house with my shoes on by mistake. Oops!
REPLY

Kathryn,
New York
Posted:
5 hours ago

6. Re: First trip to U.S.
It sounds like Americans are so informal. I'll try to be informal and polite. I hope I do the right thing. Thanks for all the advice! One more question: What's an appropriate gift for me to bring my boss and his family?
REPLY

Yong Jun Park,
Seoul
Posted:
2 hours ago

Question: Travel to Egypt
Any tips on table manners in Egypt? I'll be there on business, and I'm sure we will have business dinners. Also, anything else that's important to know?
REPLY

Sam,
Los Angeles
Posted:
4 days ago

² **hosts:** people who have visitors to the home and entertain them

1. Re: Travel to Egypt

Khalid, Cairo
Posted:
12 hours ago

Egypt is a **traditional** country, and it has many customs that are different from the U.S. Table manners are very similar to the U.S., but there are a few important differences. For instance, it's impolite to use your left hand to eat. Be sure to read about Egyptian culture before you go. You can **avoid** embarrassing yourself.

REPLY

2. Re: Travel to Egypt

Carlos, Madrid
Posted:
2 hours ago

I traveled to Egypt on business last year and saw two interesting differences in business. First, it's important to have informal conversation at the beginning of a business meeting. This is because personal relationships are very important in Egyptian business. In business meetings, American business people start with business right away. Second, during a meeting in Egypt, it's common for others to come in the room and interrupt the meeting. In the United States, important meetings rarely have interruptions, and it's rude to **interrupt** a meeting. In Egypt, these interruptions aren't rude—they're **typical**!

REPLY

MAIN IDEAS

Read the statements. Write *T* (true) or *F* (false).

_____ 1. Yong Jun Park is worried about his English.

_____ 2. It is appropriate to bring a small gift when visiting a home in the U.S.

_____ 3. Many Americans are very formal at home.

_____ 4. It's a good idea to know several different topics of conversation.

_____ 5. Khalid thinks most Egyptian customs are similar to those in the U.S.

_____ 6. Carlos thinks that business customs are the same in Egypt as they are in the U.S.

DETAILS

Write information from the forum for each of the topics below.

1. When to open gifts:

    _____

2. Good conversation topics:

    _____

3. Wearing shoes in the house:

    _____

4. Polite table manners:

    _____

5. Appropriate behavior in business meetings:

    _____

WHAT DO YOU THINK?

A. Discuss the questions in a group.

1. Why is it important for a business person to understand another culture when traveling?

2. Sun Hee writes, "Watch your American host and do what they do." Is this good advice? Why or why not?

Tip Critical Thinking

What Do You Think activities ask you to **discuss** your ideas. **Discussing** your ideas helps you to understand information better.

B. Think about both Reading 1 and Reading 2 as you discuss the questions. Then choose one question and write five to eight sentences in response.

1. What have you learned about etiquette in different cultures? Did you learn this from traveling or living in another country, or by meeting people from other cultures? Give examples.

2. Do you think that people are naturally polite? Or do they learn to be polite? Explain.

Not every word starting with *in-*, *im-*, or *un-* has a prefix meaning *not*. For example, these words do not have negative prefixes: *interrupt, impression, uncle.*

A **prefix** is a group of letters at the beginning of a word. Adding a prefix to a word changes its meaning. Understanding prefixes will help you increase your vocabulary. The prefixes *in-*, *im-*, and *un-* mean *not* and are added to adjectives.

There are no rules for when to use *-un-* or *in-*. You need to learn these words or use a dictionary to help you.

informal	not formal
invisible	not invisible
unusual	not usual
unable	not able

Im- is added to an adjective that starts with *m* or *p.*

impolite	not polite
immature	not mature

A. Look at the words below. Decide the correct prefix for each word. Then write the new words in the chart. Check your answers in the dictionary.

~~appropriate~~	clear	common
comfortable	dependable	expensive
formal	perfect	polite
possible	traditional	usual

in-	im-	un-
inappropriate		

B. Complete the sentences with words from Activity A. Use the word with or without the prefix. For some sentences, there is more than one correct answer.

1. My sister is very _____. She always does what she says she will do.

2. The directions were confusing and _____. Kenan got lost three times trying to get to the restaurant.

3. Because her first name was so _____, she always had to repeat it many times.

4. It's _____ for me to finish the project on time. I have too much research to do. I can't do it.

5. Our receptionist is very friendly and welcoming. She makes people feel _____ when they come into the office.

6. Although it was a small and _____ gift, it was very thoughtful. The cost wasn't important.

7. The customer was very _____. He was so rude that no one wanted to help him.

8. Many people send quick email invitations to parties, but Jodi sent a _____ invitation in the mail to her party. She chose beautiful expensive paper.

9. The bed was very _____, so I barely slept all night and I had a backache in the morning.

10. In the U.S. it's _____ to ask people how old they are or how much money they make.

WRITING

Supporting your main idea with examples

When you write a paragraph, you need to support your main idea. One way to support the main idea is with examples. Examples will make your ideas clear to your readers.

Writers often introduce their examples with the phrases *for example* and *for instance.*

> My advice is to know good topics of conversation. For example, you can talk about travel, food, music, or sports.

A. Read this response to Yong Jun Park's question from Reading 2, *What's an appropriate gift for me to bring my boss and his family?* What is the main idea of the response? What are the examples?

It's difficult to select the right gift to bring a host, especially if you don't know the person or the culture very well. However, there are several appropriate gifts to bring a host. For example, you can bring flowers. Buy a nice bouquet of flowers from a florist or even at the supermarket. Be sure to take the price tag off, though. Food is another good example of an appropriate item to bring. Ask the host what you can bring, or bring something everybody will probably enjoy, like a basket of fruit. If you don't want to bring food or flowers, be creative. For instance, you can bring a small gift for the home. Think of something that people use even if they already have it. Soap and hand towels are a good idea.

Main idea: _____

Examples: _____

B. Copy the topic and concluding sentences into your notebook. Then complete the paragraph. Give examples to support the main idea in the topic sentence.

Topic sentence: Many people do not have good cell phone manners, and they are impolite when they use their phones. For example,...

Concluding sentence: ...If cell phone users were more thoughtful of others, they might be more polite.

It is important to make sure that the subject and verb in a sentence agree. Use the singular form of the verb with singular subjects.

My **aunt** always **speaks** in a very loud voice.
  subject   verb

The **cake is** delicious.
  subject verb

Use the plural form of the verb with plural subjects.

Articles about business etiquette **are** very useful.
  subject   verb

My **cats eat** twice a day.
  subject verb

With *there is/there are*, the subject comes after the verb.

There **is** a lot of **information** on the Internet about manners.
  verb   subject

There **are** fifteen **students** in my class.
  verb   subject

Remember that some plural nouns do not end in *-s*. For example, *people, children, police.*

Children learn manners from their parents.
  subject verb

Tip for Success

When you edit your own writing, underline subjects and verbs in every sentence to check for subject-verb agreement.

A. Underline the subject in each sentence. Then complete the sentence with the correct form of the verb. The first one has been done for you.

1. My <u>brother</u> _____lives_____ (live) in Boston.

2. There _____ (be) a man waiting outside for you.

3. My children _____ (love) to swim.

4. The police in my neighborhood _____ (be) very helpful.

5. People _____ (use) the Internet to get all kinds of information.

6. This book _____ (give) helpful advice on how to do business in other countries.

B. Read this post from a Web page. Circle the subject and underline the verb in each sentence. Then correct the errors in subject-verb agreement.

> In my opinion, the most annoying habit is talking on cell phones. People is talking on their cell phones all the time. My brother always interrupt our conversations and answer his phone. People like my brother doesn't care about manners. People talk on cell phones in restaurants and in doctors' offices. There is times when cell phones are very annoying. Cell phones ring and interrupts our thoughts. People need to show more respect for others. There is appropriate and inappropriate places to use cell phones.

Unit Assignment | Write a paragraph with supporting examples

 In this assignment, you are going to write a paragraph in response to a question posted on an online forum about politeness. As you prepare your paragraph, think about the Unit Question, "What does it mean to be polite?" and refer to the Self-Assessment checklist on page 61.

For alternative unit assignments, see the *Q: Skills for Success Teacher's Handbook.*

PLAN AND WRITE

A. **BRAINSTORM** To get other ideas for your writing, read the following questions from an online forum. Choose which question you want to answer for your paragraph. Then freewrite your ideas about the question in your notebook.

1. I'm traveling to the United States for the first time. What do you know about manners in the U.S.? What tips do you have about being polite?

2. I think that people today are very rude. I'm the father of two young boys, ages five and ten. How can I teach my sons to be polite?

B. **PLAN** Complete the activities.

1. Write a topic sentence for your paragraph in your notebook. Your topic sentence should answer the question you chose and contain your controlling idea.

2. Write as many examples as you can in your notebook. Use your ideas from Activity A to help you.

3. Discuss your topic sentence and examples with a partner. Circle the examples that best support your topic sentence.

4. Write the question you chose in your notebook. Then list as many examples as you can.

5. Discuss your question and examples with a partner. Circle the examples that best answer and support your question.

C. **WRITE** Use your ideas from Activity B to help you write a paragraph in your notebook. Look at the Self-Assessment checklist on page 61 to guide your writing.

REVISE AND EDIT

A. **PEER REVIEW** Read your partner's paragraph. Answer these questions and discuss them with your partner.

1. Is the topic sentence clear? Does it answer the question?

2. Are there at least two examples? Put a check (✔) in the margin next to each one.

3. Are the examples clear to you? Are they introduced with a phrase like *for example* or *for instance*?

4. What additional information could you or your partner add to the paragraph?

5. Do you think that this information will be helpful to the person who asked the question? Why or why not?

B. **REWRITE** Review the answers to the questions in Activity A. You may want to revise and rewrite your paragraph.

C. EDIT Complete the Self-Assessment checklist as you prepare to write the final draft of your paragraph. Be prepared to hand in your work or discuss it in class.

Yes	No	SELF-ASSESSMENT
☐	☐	Is the first line of the paragraph indented?
☐	☐	Does each sentence start with a capital letter and end with a period or question mark?
☐	☐	Is each word spelled correctly? Check a dictionary if you are not sure.
☐	☐	Is there vocabulary from the unit in the paragraph?
☐	☐	Do you use any adjectives with prefixes? Did you use the correct prefixes?
☐	☐	Do the subjects and verbs agree?

Track Your Success

Circle the words you learned in this unit.

Nouns
advice 🔑
behavior 🔑
custom 🔑
gesture
manners
period 🔑 AWL
respect 🔑

Verbs
avoid 🔑
interrupt 🔑

Adjectives
awkward 🔑
informal 🔑
traditional 🔑 AWL
typical 🔑

Adverbs
appropriately AWL
firmly 🔑

Phrases
make a good impression
take part in

🔑 Oxford 3000™ words
AWL Academic Word List

Check (✓) the skills you learned. If you need more work on a skill, refer to the pages in parentheses.

READING ○	I can identify supporting details. (p. 49)
VOCABULARY ○	I can use prefixes correctly. (p. 55)
WRITING ○	I can support main ideas with examples. (p. 57)
GRAMMAR ○	I can use subject-verb agreement correctly. (p. 58)
LEARNING OUTCOME ○	I can write a paragraph in response to a question on an online discussion forum about politeness.

UNIT 4

Games

READING ● taking notes
VOCABULARY ● using the dictionary
WRITING ● writing an opinion paragraph
GRAMMAR ● modals

LEARNING OUTCOME

Express and support your opinion about what makes a competition unfair.

AUS

Unit QUESTION

What makes a competition unfair?

PREVIEW THE UNIT

A Discuss these questions with your classmates.

What sports do you like to play? What sports do you like to watch?

Do you prefer team sports or individual sports? Why?

Look at the photo. Where are these people? What are they doing?

B Discuss the Unit Question above with your classmates.

Listen to *The Q Classroom*, Track 11 on CD 1, to hear other answers.

C Circle the answer of the word that makes each statement true for you.

a. I (*often / sometimes / rarely*) watch sports on TV.

b. I think professional athletes' salaries are (*too high / about right / too low*).

c. I think most Olympic competitions are (*fair / unfair*).

D Look at the list of sports below. Which sports do you think are the most interesting to watch? Write the sports in order from *most interesting to watch (1)* to *least interesting to watch (8)*. Then discuss your answers with a partner.

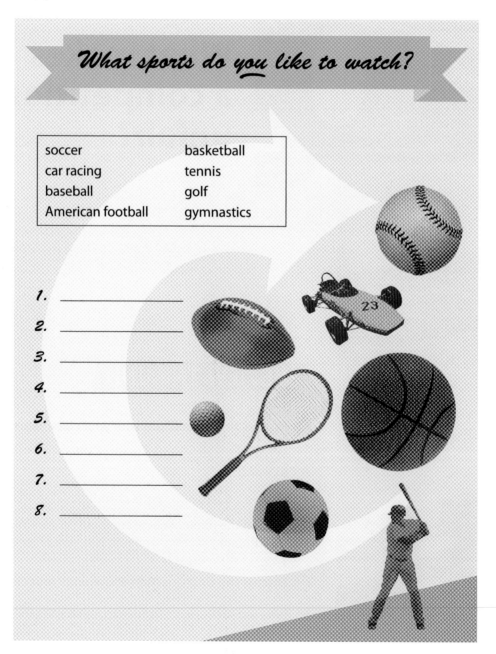

What sports do you like to watch?

soccer	basketball
car racing	tennis
baseball	golf
American football	gymnastics

1. _____
2. _____
3. _____
4. _____
5. _____
6. _____
7. _____
8. _____

READING 1 | Money and Sports

VOCABULARY

Here are some words from Reading 1. Read the sentences. Then write each bold word next to the correct definition.

1. Because he is tall for his age, Ramon has an **advantage** when he plays basketball with his friends.

2. Our baseball team was very strong last year, and we won the state **championship**.

3. When I **compete** against my brother in tennis, I usually lose.

4. Amy's new bike had an immediate **effect** on her results. She won her next three races.

5. The team's **financial** situation is very bad. They don't have enough money for new uniforms.

6. My favorite sports **include** volleyball and soccer.

7. The **limit** for the number of people allowed in the club's swimming pool is 45. It is unsafe with more than 45 people.

8. Our soccer coach had a **solution** to our problem. She had us change positions.

a. _____ (n.) a series of competitions to find the best player or team

b. _____ (adj.) connected with money

c. _____ (v.) to have someone or something as a part of the whole

d. _____ (n.) a change that is caused by something; a result

e. _____ (n.) something that helps you or that is useful

f. _____ (n.) the greatest amount of something that is possible or allowed

g. _____ (n.) the answer to a question or problem

h. _____ (v.) to try to win or achieve something

This is an article from a sports magazine that talks about money and professional soccer teams. It shows some of the effects money can have on a team's success.

Do you think wealthy teams are usually better teams?

☐ Yes ☐ No

CD 1
Track 12 **Read the article.**

Money and Sports

1 "Goal!" shouts the announcer. It is a familiar sound for Manchester United these days. They have just scored another goal against a visiting team. Compared to United, the other side looks weak. The visiting players know that it is almost impossible to win a game against Man United. Man U has better players, better coaches, better equipment, and better salaries. They have something that many teams don't have: a lot of money. This gives their club an unfair **advantage** over other teams that are not as wealthy.

2 Manchester United Football Club is the richest sports team in the world. The English club is worth more than $1.8 billion. The Spanish soccer team Real Madrid is worth $1.3 billion. These clubs have enough money to pay the high salaries of the best players in the world. For example, in 2008, Manchester United paid Cristiano Ronaldo more than $18 million. They paid Wayne Rooney more than $16 million. Other teams also spend a lot of money on their players. These wealthy clubs **include** Barcelona in Spain, AC Milan in Italy, and Chelsea in England. As a result, these teams have been very successful. For example, Manchester United won **championships** in 2006, 2008, and 2009. Money is a clear advantage for these professional teams.

3 The wealthiest teams make money in several ways. First, they can sell tickets at high prices because fans[1] want to see the top players in action. Second, television stations pay the teams to broadcast their games. Third, large companies give **financial** support to the best teams. These corporate sponsors[2] pay money so that their company name can be on the clubs' shirts, shoes, and stadiums.

4 The recent success of the English team Chelsea shows an example of the **effect** of money on a team. For many years, Chelsea was a club with little money and few wins. They didn't have a lot of money to pay good players. Their last championship win was in 1955. Everything changed in 2003, when Russian billionaire Roman Abramovich bought the team for $233 million. In his first year, Abramovich spent more than $350 million on players. By 2006, Chelsea had won two championships. Now Chelsea is one of the richest clubs in the world.

5 Many sports fans feel that money in sports creates an unfair advantage. Some teams

---

[1] **fans:** people who are very enthusiastic about something
[2] **corporate sponsors:** companies that help pay for special sports events

have so much money that it seems impossible for poorer clubs to beat them. Wealthy teams are usually more successful, so they sell more tickets and make more money. Teams that do not have as much money usually are not as successful. It is difficult for them to get money from tickets, television, and corporate sponsors. Sports fans know that money gives some clubs a great advantage.

6   There are no easy **solutions** to this problem, but there are some possibilities. Some people think that rich teams could share some of their money with the poorer ones. This way, the poorer teams would be able to pay higher salaries for better players. Another solution is to put a **limit** on the amount of money that teams can spend on players' salaries. This way, the players' salaries would not continue to rise so much. However, finding and agreeing upon the best solution is very complicated.

Sports fans love close competition between athletes.

7   Sports fans love close competitions between athletes, but everyone wants teams to **compete** fairly. Fair competitions do not seem possible when there are a small number of teams that are very wealthy. Money creates unfair advantages in professional sports, and although there are no easy answers, we should continue to search for ways to make sports fair.

Rank	Team	Country	Value ($mil)	Yearly Revenue ($mil)
1	Manchester United	England	1,870	512
2	Real Madrid	Spain	1,353	576
3	Arsenal	England	1,200	349
4	Bayern Munich	Germany	1,100	465
5	Liverpool	England	1,010	332
6	AC Milan	Italy	990	330
7	Barcelona	Spain	960	487
8	Chelsea	England	800	424
9	Juventus	Italy	600	264
10	Schalke 04	Germany	510	234

World's Richest Soccer Clubs in 2009

Note: *Value* is how much the club is worth. *Yearly Revenue* is how much the club makes every year from ticket sales, tv time, and so on.

MAIN IDEAS

Read the statements. Write _T_ (true) or _F_ (false).

_____ 1. The wealthiest teams can attract the best players.

_____ 2. The wealthiest teams are usually the most successful.

_____ 3. The wealthiest teams sell their tickets at low prices.

_____ 4. Many sports fans feel that wealthy teams have an unfair advantage.

_____ 5. There are some easy solutions to the problem of wealthy teams having an unfair advantage.

DETAILS

Answer these questions.

1. According to the article, which soccer team is the richest in the world?

   _____

2. Who received the highest salary in 2008? How much was it?

   _____

3. What do corporate sponsors do for a team?

   _____

4. In the article, what are the two suggested solutions to the problem of money in sports?

   _____

5. According to the chart, which country has four top-ranked teams?

   _____

6. According to the chart, what is the difference in value between Real Madrid and Schalke 04, in millions of dollars?

   _____

Tip for Success

Reading a graph or chart requires special attention. Read the title and think about each of the labels. Ask yourself, "What does this chart tell me?"

 **WHAT DO YOU THINK?**

Discuss the questions in a group. Then choose one question and write five to eight sentences in response.

1. What other sports have wealthy teams and poor teams? Do they have the same problems described in Reading 1?

2. Professional athletes earn very high salaries. Do you think their salaries are too high? Why or why not?

Reading Skill | **Taking notes**

When you read an article or textbook, it is helpful to **take notes** while you read. You can write notes directly in the book next to the text. Taking notes can help you remember what you read. When you take notes, you do not need to write complete sentences. You can write short phrases or even just a few words. You can also underline or highlight important information.

Some things you might note are:
- main ideas
- supporting ideas
- important names, dates, or numbers

You can use your notes for summarizing, answering questions, comparing ideas, or studying for a test.

A. Take notes on Reading 1.

1. Reread paragraph 3 in Reading 1 on page 66. Highlight or underline the main idea and three supporting ideas or make notes in the margin beside the text.

2. Reread paragraph 4 in Reading 1 on page 66. Highlight or underline the important names and numbers or make notes in the margin beside the text.

3. Reread paragraph 6 in Reading 1 on page 67. Highlight or underline the main idea and two supporting ideas or make notes in the margin beside the text.

B. Work with a partner. Compare your notes from Activity A.

READING 2 | The Fastest Man on No Legs

VOCABULARY

Here are some words from Reading 2. Read their definitions. Then complete each sentence.

> **approve** (v.) to agree to something or accept that something is allowed
>
> **ban** (v.) to officially say that something is not allowed
>
> **comment** (v.) to give your opinion or feeling
>
> **energy** (n.) strength and ability to be active without getting tired
>
> **reason** (n.) the cause of something; something that explains why something happens
>
> **success** (n.) the fact that you have achieved or done something that you want
>
> **technology** (n.) the scientific knowledge or equipment that is needed for a particular industry
>
> **train** (v.) to prepare yourself, especially for a sports event, by practicing

1. Airline companies agreed to _____ smoking on airplanes several years ago. Now smoking is not allowed on any airplanes.

2. After years of hard work, Sumiko's career as a professional golfer was a great _____. She won lots of championships and is in TV advertisements.

3. Tomas and Julio usually _____ three hours a day before a big competition.

4. The _____ for my low test score became clear: I had studied the wrong unit.

5. Last night our basketball coaches voted to _____ the new rules. They all felt the new rules were fair.

6. The player refused to _____ on his injury for the reporters. He didn't say anything about it.

7. Playing sports requires a lot of _____, so athletes need to eat healthy foods and take vitamins.

8. New _____ is helping improve sports equipment. Now athletes can ski, bike, and swim even faster.

PREVIEW READING 2

This is an article from a news magazine about an athlete, Oscar Pistorius. Pistorius is a disabled athlete who wants to compete with able-bodied athletes. After the article, you will read a letter sent to the editor of the magazine from a reader who gives an opinion about disabled and able-bodied athletes.

Do you think a disability can be an advantage? Why? Why not?

CD 1
Track 13

Read the magazine article and the letter to the editor.

The Fastest Man on No Legs

1   As South African runner Oscar Pistorius steps onto the track for a race, no one can avoid looking at his legs. They are not the usual athlete's legs, with strong, tight muscles. His legs are shiny, black, and shaped like the letter J. Instead of muscles, he has prosthetic[1] legs made of special materials. With these legs, Pistorius is becoming one of the fastest runners on earth. Pistorius is the winner of many competitions for disabled athletes, but he also wants to compete against able-bodied athletes. Including him in races against able-bodied runners is controversial.

2   When Pistorius was born in 1986, he had no legs below his knees. He has had artificial

Disabled athletes from all over the world compete in the Paralympics, a series of international contests similar to the Olympic Games.

legs since childhood, but this never stopped him from doing many different sports. Pistorius began competing as a runner in 2004. Each

---

[1] **prosthetic:** artificial

year, his prosthetic legs were lighter and better, and each year, he was able to run faster and faster. One of the keys to his **success** is his preparation and hard work. The other key to his success is his prosthetic legs, which are the most advanced in the world.

3   Pistorius dreamed of running in the 2008 Olympic Games, but in 2007, officials decided that he could not compete. They said that the Olympic Games **ban** the use of anything that gives a person an advantage over another athlete not using similar equipment. They believed that his prosthetic legs gave him an unfair advantage over able-bodied athletes. They argued that his legs were longer than the average person's legs and much lighter. Some experts believe that his prosthetic legs give him additional power.

4   Pistorius protested the decision. He wanted disabled athletes to be able to compete fairly against able-bodied athletes. In May 2008, after additional tests on his legs, officials **approved** his Olympic application. They said that his prosthetic legs did not give him an advantage. Tests showed that most of his **energy** and power come from his upper body, not his legs. Unfortunately, Pistorius wasn't fast enough in the trials[2], and he didn't compete in the 2008 Olympic Games in August.

5   Since then, Pistorius has continued to **train** for future Olympic Games. He has competed successfully in international running competitions against able-bodied athletes. For now, the rules allow him to compete against able-bodied runners. Officials have decided that he does not have an unfair advantage. However, as **technology** gives disabled athletes better prosthetic legs, arms, and hands, questions about unfair advantages will continue.

---

[2] **trials:** competitions to see who will be on the Olympic team for a country

CD 1
Track 14

Letter to the Editor

I am writing to **comment** on your article about the South African runner, Oscar Pistorius. I agree that he is a fantastic athlete, and his story is heart-warming. However, I do not think that he should compete against able-bodied athletes. I believe he has an unfair advantage. Tests showed that his prosthetic legs make him taller than his natural height. They also give him extra power. Able-bodied runners have nothing extra. They only have their bodies and their shoes. As technology improves, prosthetic legs will become better and better. With these improvements, a disabled athlete will be able to run faster and more easily. This is unfair to able-bodied athletes. In every sport, the rules must be fair. In youth sports, children compete against others of the same age. In weightlifting and boxing, athletes compete against others with the same body weight. The Paralympic Games are a special competition for disabled athletes, and in my opinion, Pistorius ought to compete in these games. For these **reasons**, I believe that disabled athletes should compete separately.

George Dutra
Hoboken, New Jersey

MAIN IDEAS

A. Read the notes for the article on pages 71–72. Write the correct paragraph number next to each note.

<u>3</u> a. Olympic officials said he had unfair advantage

___ b. Rules allow him to compete against able-bodied runners, but new technology will bring new questions

___ c. Wins races for disabled athletes; wants to compete in regular races

___ d. More tests showed no advantage; approved his application

___ e. Was always athletic; prosthetic legs better each year; legs and hard work keys to his success

B. Reread the letter to the editor on page 72. Write the main idea of the letter in one sentence. Then compare your answer with your partner.

_____

_____

DETAILS

A. Answer these questions.

1. Where is Oscar Pistorius from? _____

2. When did Pistorius begin competing as a runner? _____

3. Why did officials believe that Pistorius' legs gave him an unfair advantage?

_____

4. When officials tested his legs in May 2008, what did the tests show?

_____

5. Why didn't Pistorius compete in the 2008 Olympics?

_____

WHAT DO YOU THINK?

A. Discuss these questions in a group. Then choose one question and write five to eight sentences in response.

1. Do you think that Pistorius should be allowed to compete against able-bodied athletes? Why or why not?

2. Coaches and sports officials, including referees and judges, are responsible for making sure that athletes play by the rules. In informal games, there is no referee, judge, or coach. How do players decide what is fair?

B. Think about both Reading 1 and Reading 2 as you discuss the question.

In professional sports, when a player does something that makes the competition unfair, officials often make the player pay a large amount of money, called a fine. Do you think that a large fine is a good way to help make sports fair? Why or why not?

| Vocabulary Skill | Using the dictionary | |

Understanding additional information

A dictionary gives you more than just the definition of a word. It also gives you other useful information. For example:

- the pronunciation of the word
- the part of speech
- example sentences to show how to use the word correctly
- other forms of the word

When you read the example sentences, notice which prepositions are used with a particular verb. Notice which nouns are used with a particular adjective. Understanding additional information in a dictionary will help you learn how to use new words correctly.

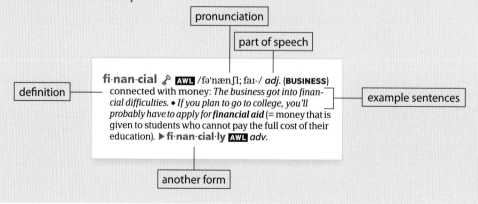

All dictionary entries are from the *Oxford American Dictionary for learners of English* © Oxford University Press 2011.

A. Read the dictionary definition below. Then answer the questions.

com·pete 🔑 /kəm'pit/ *verb* [I] **compete (against/with sb) (for sth)** to try to win or achieve something, or to try to be better than someone else: *The world's best athletes compete in the Olympic Games.* ◆ *The teams are competing for the state championship.* ◆ *When they were kids, they always used to compete with each other.* ◆ *They had to compete against several larger companies to get the contract.*

1. Which prepositions are used with the verb **compete**? _____

2. Which prepositions are used in these phrases?

    a. compete _____ or _____ a person

    b. compete _____ the championship

    c. compete _____ each other

    d. compete _____ the Olympic Games

3. Which example sentence shows that *compete* is not just for sports?

    _____

4. Using the example sentences as a guide, write two of your own sentences with *compete*.

    _____

    _____

Tip for Success

Be sure you know the abbreviations and meanings for parts of speech in a dictionary.

n. noun / *v.* verb / *adv.* adverb / *adj.* adjective / *prep.* preposition / *conj.* conjunction

B. Use your dictionary to answer these questions.

1. What part of speech is the word *responsibility*? *responsible*?

    _____ , _____

2. The word *expert* is a noun. What other part of speech can it be?

    _____

3. What parts of speech is the word *profit*? *profitable*?

    _____ and _____ , _____

4. What is the plural form of *ability*? _____

WRITING

In an **opinion paragraph**, you give your ideas about a topic. Writers often introduce their opinions with these phrases:

I (don't) think (that); I (don't) believe (that); In my opinion; I feel (that)

> **I do not think** that it is fair for poor teams to compete against wealthy teams.
> **I believe that** players should not be permitted to break the rules.

In an opinion paragraph, you want to make the reader agree with your opinion, so you need to support your opinion with **reasons** and **supporting details**, or **examples**.

> Wealthy teams can sell tickets at high prices because fans want to see the top players in action.
> Second, television stations pay the teams to broadcast their games.
> Third, large companies give support to the best teams.

Your paragraph should end with a strong **concluding sentence**. Your concluding sentence should restate the topic of your paragraph and your opinion about it.

> For these reasons, I believe that using the prosthetic limbs is unfair.
> I feel strongly that money creates an unfair advantage in sports.

Tip for Success

Phrases that introduce your opinions (*I believe that, I think that*) can make your opinions sound more polite.

A. Reread the letter to the editor on page 72. Answer the questions. Then compare your answers with a partner.

1. What four phrases does the writer use to introduce his opinions?

   _____

2. Underline the concluding sentence. Is it a restatement or a summary?

   _____

 **Critical Thinking**

In Activity B, you have to **show** your understanding of a reading text by completing a graphic organizer. **Showing** information using a graphic organizer is a good way to remember what you learn.

B. Fill in the graphic organizer with information from the letter to the editor on page 72.

Opinion

> Pistorius should not compete _____.

Reasons

> His prosthetic legs give him _____.

> _____ must be fair in all sports.

Supporting Details

> Taller, longer legs

Supporting Details

>

Grammar Modals

One way to give your opinion is to use the **modals** *should, should (not)*, and *ought to*.

> Professional athletes **should have** lower salaries.
> Coaches **ought to follow** the rules.
> I believe that disabled athletes **should not compete** against able-bodied athletes.

Note that *ought not* is rarely used.

To make a very strong statement of your opinion, you can use *must* and *must not*.

> Officials **must allow** disabled athletes to participate in the Olympic Games.
> We **must not** let sports be unfair in our schools.

A. Look at the letter to the editor on page 72. Underline the modals *should*, *ought to* and *must*.

B. Complete the first part of these sentences using *should*, *should not*, or *ought to*. Then finish the sentence with your own ideas. Use each modal at least once. Then compare and discuss your answers with a partner.

1. I think that children _____ compete in very competitive

   sports because _____.

2. Athletes _____ take drugs to improve their performance

   because _____.

3. I believe that there _____ be a limit on salaries for

   professional soccer players because _____.

4. In my opinion, athletes in schools _____ get good grades

   because _____.

Unit Assignment | **Write an opinion paragraph**

In this assignment, you will write an opinion paragraph in which you answer the question, "What makes a competition unfair?" As you prepare to write your opinion paragraph, think about the Unit Question and refer to the Self-Assessment checklist on page 80.

For alternative unit assignments, see the *Q: Skills for Success Teacher's Handbook*.

PLAN AND WRITE

Your Writing Process

For this activity you could also use Stage 1A, *Freewriting* in *Q Online Practice*.

A. BRAINSTORM Complete the activities.

1. What makes a competition unfair? Brainstorm a list of ideas.

   _____

   _____

   _____

2. Circle two or three of the best ideas on your list.

B. **PLAN** Discuss your ideas from Activity A in a group. Then write your opinions as a topic sentence for your paragraph and complete the graphic organizer with your reasons and supporting details.

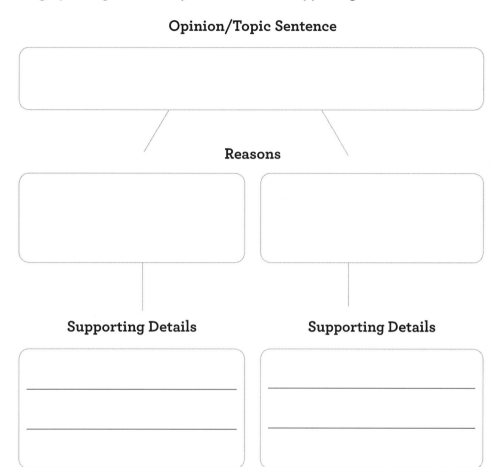

Opinion/Topic Sentence

Reasons

Supporting Details   Supporting Details

C. **WRITE** Write your paragraph in your notebook. Include phrases from the Writing Skill on page 76 to introduce your opinions. Use the modals *should* (*not*), *ought to*, and *must* to give your opinion. Be sure that your paragraph ends with a strong concluding sentence. Look at the Self-Assessment checklist on page 80 to guide your writing.

REVISE AND EDIT

A. **PEER REVIEW** Read your partner's paragraph. Answer these questions and discuss them with your partner.

1. Does the topic sentence state the opinion? What is the opinion?

2. Are there at least two clear reasons for the opinion? Are the reasons clear? Put a check (✓) next to each reason.

3. Are the two reasons supported with details? In the margin, put a plus sign (+) next to each supporting detail.

4. Is there a strong concluding sentence?

B. **REWRITE** Review the answers to the questions in Activity A. You may want to revise and rewrite your paragraph.

C. **EDIT** Complete the Self-Assessment checklist as you prepare to write the final draft of your paragraph. Be prepared to hand in your work or discuss it in class.

SELF-ASSESSMENT		
Yes	No	
☐	☐	Is the first line of the paragraph indented?
☐	☐	Does each sentence start with a capital letter and end with a period or question mark?
☐	☐	Is each word spelled correctly? Check a dictionary if you are not sure.
☐	☐	Do the subjects and verbs agree?
☐	☐	Is there vocabulary from the unit in the paragraph?
☐	☐	Underline any modals. Is the base form of a verb used after the modal?

Track Your Success

Circle the words you learned in this unit.

Nouns
advantage 🔑
championship
effect 🔑
energy 🔑 AWL
limit 🔑
reason 🔑

solution 🔑
success 🔑
technology 🔑 AWL

Verbs
approve 🔑
ban 🔑
comment 🔑 AWL

compete 🔑
include 🔑
train 🔑

Adjectives
financial 🔑 AWL

🔑 Oxford 3000™ words
AWL Academic Word List

Check (✓) the skills you learned. If you need more work on a skill, refer to the pages in parentheses.

READING ●	I can take notes. (p. 69)
VOCABULARY ●	I can use the dictionary to learn additional information about a word. (p. 74)
WRITING ●	I can write an opinion paragraph. (p. 76)
GRAMMAR ●	I can use modals correctly. (p. 77)
LEARNING OUTCOME ●	I can express and support my opinion about what makes a competition unfair.

UNIT

5

Family Ties

READING	•	skimming
VOCABULARY	•	using the dictionary
WRITING	•	using correct personal letter format
GRAMMAR	•	comparative and superlative adjectives

LEARNING OUTCOME

Write a personal letter describing a new family business.

Unit QUESTION

What makes a family business successful?

PREVIEW THE UNIT

(A) Discuss these questions with your classmates.

Do you know anyone who owns a family business? What kind of business is it? Do you think it's successful?

Would you like to work in a business with your family? Explain.

Look at the photo. Who are the people? Where are they?

(B) Discuss the Unit Question above with your classmates.

Listen to *The Q Classroom*, Track 15 on CD 1, to hear other answers.

PREVIEW THE UNIT

C Look at the photos. Match the letter of the photo with the correct quotation. Then discuss the meaning of each quotation with your classmates.

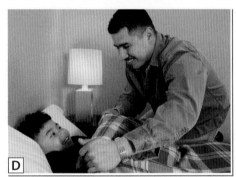

_____ 1. The family that plays together, stays together. — *Common proverb*

_____ 2. True happiness is three generations living under one roof. — *Chinese proverb*

_____ 3. A man should never neglect his family for business. — *Walt Disney*

_____ 4. It's more important to know where your children are tonight than where your ancestors were a hundred years ago. — *Anonymous*

D Discuss these questions with a partner.

1. Do you or did you play games with your family? Do you know any families that play games together?

2. Do you know any families that have three generations (children, parents, grandparents) living in the same house? How do they get along?

3. Do you know any people who put their work before their families? How does this affect the families?

READING 1 | Family Unity Builds Success

VOCABULARY

Here are some words from Reading 1. Read their definitions. Then complete each sentence.

corporation (*n.*) a big company

courage (*n.*) not being afraid, or not showing that you are afraid when you do something dangerous or difficult

design (*v.*) to plan and develop how something will look

expand (*v.*) to become bigger, or make something become bigger

expert (*n.*) a person who knows a lot about something

manage (*v.*) to control someone or something

strength (*n.*) a good quality or ability that someone or something has

unity (*n.*) a situation in which people are working together or in agreement

1. Danilo and Katia showed a lot of _____ when they left their country to open a business in France.

2. We hired an artist to help us _____ our new home.

3. Mr. Gibbs is a(n) _____ on restaurant management. He has managed restaurants for 20 years and has written a book on the subject.

4. The Smiths have a strong sense of _____ in their family. They always take care of each other.

5. Our business only has six employees now, but we think it will _____ a lot over the next few years.

6. Pablo's greatest _____ is his ability to keep a positive attitude when times are difficult.

7. Ford, a car company, is an extremely large _____.

8. Ms. Lee is a great teacher. I don't know how she can _____ all of those children.

Skimming is reading a text quickly to get the general idea of what it is about. Skimming is useful when you read a newspaper or magazine, read online, or take a test. When you do research, you skim an article to see if it will be useful. When you skim, use these tips.

- Read the title.
- Quickly read the first sentence of each paragraph.
- Move your eyes quickly through the text.
- Do not read every sentence or every word.
- If the text is short, read the first and last sentence of each paragraph.

A. Take one minute to skim Reading 1 on pages 87–88. As you read, underline the first sentence of each paragraph.

B. Write what you can remember about the reading in your notebook.

C. Take one minute to skim Reading 2 on pages 91–92. Then look at the chart below. Check (✓) which reading has information about each topic.

Which reading has information about...	Reading 1	Reading 2
1. a family that owned a newspaper	☐	☑
2. a restaurant business	☐	☐
3. family businesses in the United States	☐	☐
4. a family business owned by immigrants	☐	☐
5. difficulties with family businesses	☐	☐

PREVIEW READING 1

This is an article from a business magazine. It shows how a family started a successful restaurant. Over time, they expanded their business and included more family members. What advantages do you think there are to having a family business?

Family Unity Builds Success

1   *When her five daughters were young, Helene An always told them that there was* **strength** *in* **unity**. *To show this, she held up one chopstick, representing one person. Then she easily broke it into two pieces. Next, she tied several chopsticks together, representing a family. She showed the girls it was hard to break the tied chopsticks. This lesson about family unity stayed with the daughters as they grew up.*

2   Helene An and her family own a multi-million-dollar restaurant business in California. However, when Helene and her husband Danny left their home in Vietnam in 1975, they didn't have much money. They moved their family to San Francisco. There they joined Danny's mother, who owned a small Italian sandwich shop. The Ans began with only a small idea and never dreamed of the success they have today.

3   Soon after the Ans' arrival in the United States, Helene and her mother-in-law, Diana, changed the sandwich shop into a small Vietnamese restaurant. They named it Green Dragon, which symbolizes good luck in Vietnam. The restaurant was very popular, and they **expanded** from 20 seats to 70. The five daughters helped work in the restaurant when they were young. Their mother told them that they all had to work hard to reach their goals and make their family stronger. Helene did not want her daughters to always work in the family business because she thought it was too hard.

4   Eventually the girls all graduated from college and went away to work for themselves, but one by one, the daughters returned to work in the family business. They opened new restaurants in San Francisco and in Beverly Hills, a wealthy area in Los Angeles. The daughters chose new names and styles for their restaurants. Over the years, some ideas were successful, but others were not. Even though family members sometimes disagreed with each other, they worked together to make the business successful. Daughter Elizabeth explains, "Our mother taught us that to succeed we must have unity, and to have unity we must have peace. Without the strength of the family, there is no business. So even when we don't agree, we are willing to try a new idea."

The An family restaurant, Green Dragon

5   Their expanding business became a large **corporation** in 1996, with three generations of Ans working together. Helene is the **expert** on cooking. Helene's husband Danny An is good at making decisions. Their daughter Hannah is good with computers. Hannah's husband Danny Vu is good at thinking of new ideas and doing research.

Helene An and her daughters

Hannah's sister Elizabeth is the family artist. She **designs** the insides of the restaurants. Their sister Monique is good at **managing**.

Elizabeth says, "If you're going to work as a family, you have to know what you're good at. We work well together because we have different strengths." Even the grandchildren help out.

6   Now the Ans' corporation makes more than $20 million each year. Although they began with a small restaurant, they had big dreams, and they worked together. Now they are a big success. Helene says, "In Vietnam, I didn't have to do anything for myself. Here, I've had to do everything. But I was never unhappy because every day I could see all the members of my family, and that gave me **courage** to do more. This has been our greatest fortune[1], to work together as a family."

---

[1] **fortune:** good luck

MAIN IDEAS

Circle the answer to each question.

1. What is the main idea of paragraph 1?
   a. Family businesses can have problems.
   b. There is strength in working together as a family.
   c. Only family businesses are successful.

2. What is the main idea of paragraph 5?
   a. By 1996, their business was a large corporation.
   b. Different family members have strengths that help the business.
   c. The family members don't know what they are good at.

3. What is the main idea of the entire article?
   a. Any family can become a big success.
   b. Family members have different strengths.
   c. A family that has unity can be successful.

DETAILS

A. Write the number of the paragraph that contains the detail.

____ a. After college, the daughters returned to work in the family business.

____ b. The Ans' company makes more than $20 million each year.

____ c. Helene and Danny An left Vietnam in 1975 with no money.

____ d. The business became a corporation in 1996.

____ e. The An daughters worked in the restaurant when they were young.

B. Match each family member with the correct skill.

_e_ 1. Helene   a. managing

____ 2. Danny An   b. design

____ 3. Hannah   c. making decisions

____ 4. Danny Vu   d. computers

____ 5. Monique   e. cooking

____ 6. Elizabeth   f. new ideas and research

WHAT DO YOU THINK?

Discuss the questions in a group. Then choose one question and write five to eight sentences in response.

1. The An family members respect each other. How does this help them have a successful business?

2. What qualities do you have that can help you when working with a group of people?

READING 2 | Family Businesses

VOCABULARY

Here are some words from Reading 2. Read the sentences. Circle the answer that best matches the meaning of each bold word or phrase.

1. For many parents, communicating with their teenage children can be a big **challenge**. At this age children may not want to talk to their parents about their problems.
   a. an exciting event
   b. a difficult thing that makes you try hard

2. Mario will be a great sports reporter because of his great **enthusiasm** for sports.
   a. difficulty with something
   b. strong feeling of liking something

3. My children **depend on** me to drive them to school.
   a. need someone to provide something
   b. help someone

4. Oliver's store isn't making much money. He's worried that it's going to **fail**.
   a. be unsuccessful
   b. break the law

5. Ahmed's **goals** for the future do not include joining the family business.
   a. things that you want to do
   b. subjects that you study

6. Paula is spending more time with her friends and less time studying. Her father is worried about her change in **lifestyle**.
   a. the way that you dress
   b. the way that you live

7. My grandmother will **pass down** her jewelry to my mother.
   a. give something to a younger person
   b. create something

8. Jack still thinks he's going to become a basketball star. He needs to be more **realistic** about his career.
   a. interested and excited
   b. understanding what is possible

Tip for Success

When you are skimming a text, use a pencil tip to help your eyes move quickly across the text, or place a piece of paper under each line as your read. This will help you avoid stopping to read every word.

9. Carl's **responsibility** at home is taking out the garbage. His brother has to set the table for dinner.
   a. things that you must buy
   b. jobs or duties that you must do

10. My cousin has a **talent** for singing. She sings very beautifully.
    a. natural skill or ability
    b. thing you want

PREVIEW READING 2

This is an article from a textbook that discusses some of the problems with family businesses. It uses the example of the Bancroft family, former owners of *The Wall Street Journal*.

Skim the reading. Which paragraph discusses passing a business to the next generation?

 CD 1 Track 17   **Read the article.**

The Challenge of Running a Family Business

1   In the United States, families own about 85 percent of all businesses. However, less than 30 percent of these companies last more than 20 years. The companies **fail**, and the owners can't **pass down** the family businesses to their sons and daughters. Why is it so difficult for family businesses to survive?

2   One reason may be changing times. Fifty years ago, many families owned local grocery stores. But today, small family-owned stores cannot compete with large supermarket chains. Today, most Mom and Pop stores[1] are a thing of the past[2]. The way of life is another **challenge** in a family business. A successful company requires hard work and long hours. Younger generations may not want this **lifestyle**.

Less than 30 percent of family businesses last more than 20 years.

They may want more freedom. In addition, sons and daughters may not have the same **enthusiasm** for the business as their parents.

3   A successful family business **depends on** the family's strengths and **talents**. However,

[1] **Mom and Pop stores:** stores owned by a family or individual, not a corporation
[2] **thing of the past:** something that no longer exists

The Wall Street Journal

families also bring their weaknesses and personal problems to the workplace. Many families do not communicate well, and they are not good at solving problems together. These challenges often cause businesses to fail. According to Professor Randel Carlock, these problems are common. He says, "Being part of a family is very difficult. Being part of a family business is even more difficult." Love is important in a family, but love is not enough to run a family business. The business must achieve financial success.

4   The Bancroft family is an interesting example. For 105 years, the Bancroft family owned *The Wall Street Journal*. It is one of the most famous newspapers in the United States. But there were many family problems. They did not communicate well, and they disagreed about many things. One person said that they couldn't even agree on where to go for lunch! The younger family members wanted the business to be more profitable. The older members thought the quality of the paper was more important than making money. In addition, the family let people outside of the family manage the newspaper. They did not take part in many important decisions. Finally, in 2007, all 33 of the Bancroft family owners agreed to sell the company. Although the business had lasted several generations, the Bancrofts eventually had to sell their company because they did not manage it well. In the end, many of their family relationships suffered.

5   Many families dream of passing down their businesses to the next generation, but this requires careful planning and preparation. Good management is a key to success. All employees, especially family members, need to have clear **responsibilities**. Family business owners need to think about how decisions are made. Also, they should be **realistic** about the dreams and **goals** of the younger generation. Family businesses can be successful because of strong family ties[3]. But to succeed for more than one generation, families need to manage their businesses carefully.

[3] **ties:** something that connects you with a particular group of people

Main Ideas

A. Read the statements. Write *T* (true) or *F* (false). Then correct each false statement to make it true.

_____ 1.   Few family businesses are passed down to the next generation.

_____ 2.   Most family businesses succeed because the members love each other.

_____ 3.   Most family businesses have similar problems.

_____ 4.   Most owners of family businesses don't want to pass down the businesses to their sons and daughters.

B. Answer the question.

According to the article, how can a family business be successful?

_____

DETAILS

A. Look back at paragraph 1 in Reading 2 to find the missing information for the sentences below. Then complete each sentence.

1. In the United States, families own about ___ percent of all businesses.

2. However, less than ___ percent of these businesses last more than

   ___ years.

B. Look back at Reading 2 to find the reasons why family businesses fail. Write two of the reasons below. Then compare your answers with a partner.

1. _____

2. _____

 ## WHAT DO YOU THINK?

A. Discuss the questions in a group.

1. Reading 2 gives some reasons why family businesses fail. What other reasons can you think of?

2. What kind of people do you think can build a successful family business?

Tip Critical Thinking

The first question of Activity B asks you to **analyze** the reasons why one family was successful and the other was not. **Analyzing** is breaking information down into smaller parts so that you can understand it better.

B. Think about both Reading 1 and Reading 2 as you discuss the questions. Then choose one question and write five to eight sentences in response.

1. Why do you think that the An family was successful in their business, but the Bancroft family had to sell their business?

2. What advice would you give to someone who was thinking of starting a business?

Understanding grammatical information in the dictionary

When you look up a word in the dictionary, pay attention to the grammatical information. In addition to the part of speech, an entry will also tell you:

- if a noun is countable (C) or uncountable (U)
- if the plural of a noun has an irregular form
- if an adjective or adverb has an irregular comparative form
- if a verb has an irregular form

Looking up and understanding grammatical information about a new word helps you use it correctly.

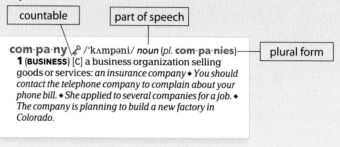

All dictionary entries are from the *Oxford American Dictionary for learners of English* © Oxford University Press 2011.

A. Use your dictionary to answer these questions.

1. Which words are uncountable? Circle them.

information	police	luggage
news	advantage	advice
planet	happiness	furniture
darkness	traffic	participant

2. What is the plural form of each of these nouns?

   a. life _____

   b. child _____

   c. cactus _____

   d. analysis _____

3. What is the simple past form of each of these phrases?

   a. break down _____

   b. burst into _____

   c. shine at _____

WRITING

Writing Skill   Using correct personal letter format

A **personal letter** is a thoughtful way of communicating with family and friends. Personal letters are usually informal, but use a standard format. These are the main sections of personal letters.

Heading:

The heading goes at the top of the page. It includes your address and the date.

    578 Oak St.
    Clewiston, FL 33440
    August 3, 2010

Greeting:

The greeting includes the name of the person you are writing to and ends with a comma.

    Dear Nora,   Hello Nora,   Hi Nora,

Body:

The body is the main text of your letter. It includes the information you want to give. The body often begins with a question.

    How are you? How is your family? I hope that you're having a nice summer
    and you enjoyed your trip to Greece…

Closing:

The closing includes one or two words and ends with a comma. Choose the appropriate closing for the person you are writing.

    Take care,   Warm regards,   Fondly,   Love,   Yours truly,   Best wishes,

A. Look at the letter to see how it is organized. Write *heading, greeting, body,* and *closing* next to the correct section of the letter.

---

578 Oak St.
Clewiston, FL 33440
August 3, 2010

Dear Ethan,

    How are you? Are you still working as a computer engineer? I hope that your family is healthy and happy. I'm sorry that I haven't written you for several months.

A formal letter has a different format. You can find information about formal letters and samples in your dictionary, your library, or online.

I'm writing because I have exciting news about our new family business. As you know, Clewiston doesn't have a sporting goods store. The closest place to buy sports equipment is about 30 miles from here. My brother Mark and I will open a sporting goods store that will be easier for residents to get to. It will have better customer service than the other store does, and our prices will be lower. Mark will be the store manager because he is good with people, and he is calmer than I am. I will be the advertising manager and do the accounting. Right now, we are all very busy. We plan to open the store in May.

I hope that you can come and visit us and our store soon! Please give my regards to your family. I look forward to hearing from you soon.

Take care,
Lucy

B. Write the heading, greeting, and first paragraph of a letter to a relative or a friend using correct letter format from Activity A in your notebook. Be sure to include a question about the person's life and something about your life.

Grammar | Comparative and superlative adjectives

Comparative adjectives describe the difference between two things.

For adjectives with one syllable, use **adjective + er**. *Than* often follows comparative adjectives.

tall	→	taller
safe	→	safer
big	→	bigger

If an adjective ends in one vowel and one consonant, double the consonant, as in *big → bigger*. If the adjective ends in -*e*, just add -*r*.

For most adjectives with two or more syllables, use **more + adjective**.

| common | → | more common |
| traditional | → | more traditional |

For two-syllable adjectives that end in -*le*, add -*r*.

| simple | → | simpler |

For two-syllable adjectives that end in -y, change the -y to i and add -er.

pretty   →   prettier
funny   →   funnier

Superlative adjectives describe three or more things.

For most adjectives that have one syllable, use **the + adjective + -est**.

tall   →   the tallest
big   →   the biggest
safe   →   the safest

For two-syllable adjectives that end in -le, use **the** and add –st.

simple   →   the simplest

For two-syllable adjectives that end in -y, change the y to i, use **the** and add -est.

pretty   →   the prettiest
funny   →   the funniest

For most adjectives with two or more syllables, add **the + most + adjective**.

informal   →   the most informal
realistic   →   the most realistic
traditional   →   the most traditional

Note: Some adjectives are irregular.

good   →   better   →   the best
bad   →   worse   →   the worst

A. Look at paragraph 2 of the letter on pages 95–96. Underline the comparatives and superlatives.

1. How many comparatives are there? _____

2. How many superlatives are there? _____

3. Which comparative is irregular? _____

4. Look at the adjectives from the letter in the chart below. Complete the chart with the missing forms of each adjective.

Adjective	Comparative	Superlative
healthy	healthier	the healthiest
exciting		
		the closest
	easier	
	better	the best
	calmer	
busy		
	lower	

B. Complete each sentence with the correct comparative form of the adjective in parentheses.

1. I'm _____ (successful) in school than my brother is.

2. Sandra is _____ (responsible) with her money than her younger sister is.

3. Elephants are _____ (intelligent) than fish.

4. People in small towns are often _____ (friendly) than people in big cities.

5. The subway is _____ (fast) than the bus.

6. Chan's goals for the future are _____ (realistic) than Brendan's.

C. Complete each sentence below with the correct superlative form of the adjective in parentheses and your own opinions. Then discuss your answers with a partner.

1. _____Ice hockey_____ is _the most interesting_ (interesting) sport to watch.

2. _____ is _____ (delicious) food in the world.

3. _____ is _____ (beautiful) season of the year.

4. _____ is _____ (difficult) sport to play.

5. _____ is _____ (famous) place in my country.

6. _____ is _____ (successful) company in the world.

In this assignment you will write a personal letter to a friend about a new family business you create. Your letter will include information about your new business and what jobs the members of your family will have. As you prepare to write your personal letter, think about the Unit Question, "What makes a family business successful?" and refer to the Self-Assessment checklist on page 100.

For alternative unit assignments, see the *Q: Skills for Success Teacher's Handbook*.

PLAN AND WRITE

A. **BRAINSTORM** Freewrite to brainstorm ideas for your new family business. Think about what jobs the members of your family will do. Write down as many ideas as you can.

_____

_____

_____

_____

_____

B. **PLAN** Review your freewriting. Choose the business you want to write about. Then answer these questions in your notebook.

1. What kind of business will it be? What kind of product or service will your business provide?

2. Describe the store or service.

3. Who will your customers be?

4. Why will your business be different from others?

5. Which family members will work at your store? What will their jobs be?

6. What are some possible difficulties you think you might have?

7. Why do you think your business will be successful?

 **Your Writing Process**

For this activity you could also use Stage 1B, *Writing an Informal Outline* in *Q Online Practice*.

C. **WRITE** Write your personal letter in your notebook. Follow the format in the Writing Skill on page 95. You do not need to include all of the details about your new business, only the most important ones. Look at the Self-Assessment checklist on page 100 to guide your writing.

REVISE AND EDIT

A. **PEER REVIEW** Read a partner's letter. Answer the questions and discuss them with your partner.

1. Does the letter clearly explain the idea for a new family business?

2. Does your partner give reasons why the new business will be successful? In the margin, put a plus sign (+) next to each reason.

3. Is there something you want to know more about? Write two questions that you have about your partner's ideas.

4. Is the letter in the correct format (heading, greeting, body, and closing)? If not, which parts are incorrect?

B. **REWRITE** Review the answers to the questions in Activity A. You may want to revise and rewrite your letter.

C. **EDIT** Complete the Self-Assessment checklist as you prepare to write the final draft of your letter. Be prepared to hand in your work or discuss it in class.

Yes	No	SELF-ASSESSMENT
☐	☐	Is the first line of the paragraph indented?
☐	☐	Does each sentence start with a capital letter and end with a period or question mark?
☐	☐	Do the subjects and verbs agree?
☐	☐	Is each word spelled correctly? Check a dictionary if you are not sure.
☐	☐	Is there vocabulary from the unit in the paragraph?
☐	☐	Underline any comparatives or superlatives. Are they the correct form?

Track Your Success

Circle the words you learned in this unit.

Nouns
challenge 🔑 AWL
corporation AWL
courage 🔑
expert 🔑 AWL
enthusiasm 🔑
goal 🔑 AWL
lifestyle
responsibility 🔑

strength 🔑
talent 🔑
unity

Verbs
design 🔑 AWL
expand 🔑 AWL
fail 🔑
manage 🔑

Adjectives
realistic 🔑

Phrasal Verbs
depend on 🔑
pass down

🔑 Oxford 3000™ words
AWL Academic Word List

Check (✓) the skills you learned. If you need more work on a skill, refer to the pages in parentheses.

READING	○	I can skim. (p. 86)
VOCABULARY	○	I can use the dictionary to understand grammatical information. (p. 94)
WRITING	○	I can write a personal letter. (pp. 95–96)
GRAMMAR	○	I can use comparative and superlative adjectives correctly. (pp. 96–97)
LEARNING OUTCOME	○	I can write a personal letter describing a new family business.

UNIT 6

Self-Reliance

READING ● identifying the author's purpose
VOCABULARY ● using the dictionary
WRITING ● describing a process
GRAMMAR ● infinitives of purpose

Here you should...
Check in
Print your boarding pass

Hello, please
check in here

LEARNING OUTCOME

Describe the steps of a process performed by either a person or a machine.

Unit QUESTION

Do you prefer to get help from a person or a machine?

PREVIEW THE UNIT

(A) Discuss these questions with your classmates.

What are some of the advantages of getting help from machines and technology?

What are some of the advantages of getting help from people instead of machines and technology?

Look at the photo. What do you see?

(B) Discuss the Unit Question above with your classmates.

Listen to *The Q Classroom*, Track 2 on CD 2, to hear other answers.

C **Look at the photos and answer the questions with a partner.**

A

Touch-screen ordering kiosk

B

Airport check-in kiosk

C

Self-service check-out

D

Photo processing kiosk

1. Which of these self-service machines have you used?

2. How does each of these self-service machines save time?

3. What problems could you have with each machine?

4. Which machine is the most useful? The least useful?

D **Discuss these questions with your classmates.**

1. How many students have used each machine in Activity C?

2. What other self-service machines do you and your classmates sometimes use?

READING

VOCABULARY

Here are some words from Reading 1. Read their definitions. Then complete each sentence.

> **automatically** (*adv.*) done in a way (like a machine) that does not require human control
> **benefit** (*n.*) advantages or good or useful effects of something
> **blame** (*v.*) to think or say that someone is responsible for something bad that happened
> **decrease** (*v.*) to become or to make something smaller or less
> **error** (*n.*) a mistake
> **estimate** (*v.*) to calculate the size, cost, or amount of something approximately
> **interact** (*v.*) to communicate or mix with
> **provide** (*v.*) to give or supply something to somebody
> **stressed** (*adj.*) feeling worried or unable to relax
> **unique** (*adj.*) unlike anything else; being the only one of its type

1. A _____ of having a laptop computer is that you can use it almost anywhere.

2. At the bank, a machine _____ sorts coins and counts them.

3. I thought I made many mistakes on the test, but later I found out that I had made only one _____.

4. I am waiting for prices to _____ before I buy a new laptop.

5. Some people _____ the changes in climate on pollution.

6. Can you give me a(n) _____ of how many people will be at the meeting?

7. My brother is good with children. He likes to _____ with them.

8. Last year I felt very _____ about my schoolwork. This year, I have fewer classes, and I feel more relaxed.

9. The school librarians are very helpful. They _____ us with a lot of useful information.

10. Instead of a typical birthday cake, Sue made a _____ and colorful one.

PREVIEW READING 1

 for Success

Before you read a text, look at the title, photos, and format of the text. Think about what kind of information it might contain.

This is a business memo from a restaurant manager to the servers. It gives the servers information about a new form of technology the restaurant is going to use.

What do you think the new technology will be in the restaurant? More than one answer is possible.

☐ Customers will pay their own bills using a credit card at a computer monitor.

☐ Customers will enter their order at their table using a computer monitor.

☐ Customers will use their cell phones to order at their table.

CD 2
Track 3

Read the memo.

Restaurant Z
Memo

DATE: May 3
TO: Servers
FROM: Mark McCormick, Dining Room Manager
RE: New touch-screen ordering

1   At Restaurant Z, we are known as a cool, trendy place for people who want a very special experience. We are always looking for better ways to serve our customers and make their experience **unique**. Next month, we will make a change so that we can really stand out[1]: touch-screen ordering, also known as "digital dining." You need to know about this new technology.

2   This is how it works: Each table will have its own tabletop computer monitor with a touch screen. Customers can view the menu on the monitor, including descriptions and photos. To start, the customer inserts her credit card and puts in her order by touching the screen. Then the program **automatically** makes suggestions for additional items to order,

[1] **stand out:** to be different

such as appetizers[2] and drinks. When the customer is ready, she pushes a button to send the order directly to the computer in the kitchen. Won't that make your job as a server easier? All you have to do is bring the food to the table when it's ready! Finally, paying the bill is quick and easy because the customer can do it herself. This exciting new technology will improve our customers' dining experience and increase your tips!

3 Now you may want to know how this change will affect you. Maybe you are afraid of losing your job. Let me assure you: you won't. In fact, you will be able to serve more customers every night! These high-tech computers not only look cool, they **decrease** the number of tasks you have to do. Hopefully, that means that you can serve more tables without feeling **stressed**!

4 Here are some questions and answers:

Q: *What are the **benefits** for me as a server?*

A: First of all, with digital dining, customers can order quickly. We will be able to serve more customers in less time. Also, the computer program will automatically suggest additional items to order. Research shows that when this happens, customers order more. We **estimate** that customer bills will be 15 to 20 percent higher. With more customers ordering more items, you will earn more money in tips. In addition, you won't have to repeat the same information over and over like a robot[3]. Finally, customers can't **blame** you for **errors** in their order—they place their own orders! Won't that be nice?

Q: *Will customers really want to do their own ordering?*

A: Yes, I think that most of our customers will love it! If a diner prefers the traditional service, we will **provide** it. But these monitors will be so much fun that everyone will want to use them! The photographs will be fantastic and the descriptions will be mouth-watering. As you know, most of our customers are tech-savvy[4], and they enjoy **interacting** with the latest gadgets[5]!

Q: *What other features will these tabletop monitors have?*

A: They'll have entertaining games and high-speed Internet access. Customers can send messages to friends and post photos of themselves at the table.

5 We will be having an employee training session to show you how digital dining works next Tuesday from 9:30–11:00 a.m. I look forward to showing you this fabulous new system!

---

[2] **appetizer:** a small amount of food that you eat as the first part of a meal
[3] **robot:** an automated machine that can do work that a person does
[4] **tech-savvy:** having knowledge and understanding of technology
[5] **gadget:** a small machine or tool

MAIN IDEAS

Circle the answer to each question.

1. What is the main reason the restaurant is going to use digital dining?
   a. to provide better service to customers
   b. to help servers get larger tips
   c. to be trendy and popular

2. What was the manager's reason for writing the second paragraph?
   a. to tell how digital dining will increase sales
   b. to explain how digital dining works
   c. to describe how customers will pay their bills

3. What is the main idea of the question and answer section?
   a. Someday monitors will replace servers.
   b. Monitors will make servers and customers happy.
   c. Customers will order more food.

DETAILS

Complete each statement with information from the memo.

1. The date of the memo is _____.

2. The restaurant will start using tabletop monitors

   _____.

3. In addition to descriptions of menu items, the monitor will show

   _____.

4. When a customer places an order, the computer program will recommend

   _____.

5. Customers' bills will be _____ when they use

   digital dining.

6. The training meeting will be _____.

 **WHAT DO YOU THINK?**

Discuss the questions in a group. Then choose one question and write five to eight sentences in response.

1. The manager mentions many of the benefits of the new monitors. What do you think some of the disadvantages or problems might be?

2. At Restaurant Z, who do you think will benefit the most from the new digital dining technology: the customers or the servers?

3. Have you ever used technology like this in a restaurant? If so, describe your experience and tell what happened. If not, would you like to use this technology? Why or why not?

| Reading Skill | Identifying the author's purpose | |

The **purpose** of a text is the reason why the author writes it. For example, the purpose of a newspaper article is to inform or give the reader information about something. The purpose of a letter to the newspaper is usually to express an opinion about something. As you read, look at the words the author uses and ask yourself questions to help you identify the purpose. Here are some questions you can ask yourself as you read:

- Is the author trying to give me information about something?
- Is the author expressing his or her opinion about something?
- Is the author telling me a personal story?
- Is the author trying to make me interested or excited about something?
- Is the author trying to make me laugh?

Identifying the author's purpose can help you better understand the text you are reading.

A. Look back at Reading 1 on pages 106–107. What is the author's purpose? Circle two answers.

a. to tell a story

b. to make someone laugh

c. to give information

d. to make someone excited about something

B. Read the titles below. Look at the words the authors use. Then match each title with the correct purpose. Compare your answers with a partner.

____ 1. "My Embarrassing Adventures with Social Networking"   a. to tell a story

____ 2. "Competitive Sports Are Too Competitive"   b. to make someone laugh

____ 3. "My Grandfather's Childhood in Egypt"   c. to express an opinion

____ 4. "New Research Shows Birds See More Colors"   d. to make someone interested in something

____ 5. "You Can Be Stronger in Two Weeks!"   e. to give information

READING 2 | I Hate Machines!

VOCABULARY

Here are some words from Reading 2. Read their definitions. Then complete each sentence.

---

access (*n.*) a way to enter a place or to use something

assist (*v.*) to help someone

connection (*n.*) a path of communication for a telephone or Internet

eventually (*adv.*) after a long time

frustrated (*adj.*) angry or impatient because you cannot do or achieve what you want to do

furious (*adj.*) very angry

install (*v.*) to put a new thing in its place so it is ready to use

on hold (*prepositional phrase*) waiting on the phone to talk to someone or continue a conversation

scan (*v.*) to pass light over a picture or document in order to copy it and put it in the memory of a computer

transfer (*v.*) to connect a telephone caller to another person or line

---

1. I thought my friends would never come back from the store, but

_____ they did.

2. Ana called, but I couldn't hear her because my phone had a bad

    _____.

3. This key will give you _____ to my apartment whenever

    you want.

4. At our store the computer specialists _____ customers.

    It's their job.

5. I'm not able to answer your question, but I can _____ you

    to a manager who can help you.

6. You don't need to type the price into the cash register. You can just

    _____ the item with this machine.

7. I tried to register for classes today, but the website didn't work! Now all

    the classes I want are full. I'm so _____.

8. I hung up after I was _____ for 30 minutes.

9. My friend damaged my new car, and then she lied to me about what

    happened. I was _____!

10. A man came to my apartment to _____ my new dishwasher.

PREVIEW READING 2

You are going to read part of a blog. A blog is a website with posts, or short essays. Blogs are usually informal and personal. Bloggers, people who create blogs, often write about their experiences, giving their opinions about various topics. Often readers add their comments and reactions. Look at the title of the blog post that follows. What do you think that the reading will be about?

I Hate Machines!

Home   Log in

Trouble with Technology

TUESDAY, MARCH 2

About

Links

Archives
January
February
March
April
May
June
July
August
September
October
November
December

1   Recently, I moved to a new apartment right across the street from my old one. I thought it would be simple to get my phone and DSL[1] line started. The technician[2] from the phone company came to **install** my telephone line. He said that I would be able to use the Internet on the same line. After he left, I discovered that the phone worked, but the DSL **connection** for the Internet didn't. So I called the phone company. Of course, I didn't get to talk to a real person. Instead, an automated voice recording asked me a lot of questions. Then I had to wait for half an hour to talk to a real person. While I was **on hold**, every few minutes a recording said, "Remember, you can use our convenient website to solve most of your problems." "Arrrrghh!!" I said to the recording, feeling **frustrated.** "Why do you think I'm calling you? I don't have a connection to the Internet."

2   I finally got to talk to a real person, but then she **transferred** me back into the automated system again. I couldn't get any help. I called a different number, and the person told me to be at my house for a technician to come the next day. I stayed home from work, but nobody came! I called them again. The recording said, "We're sorry, all agents are busy **assisting** other customers. We are unable to take your call." Then the machine hung up on me. Three days later, I received a phone call from them. But again, it wasn't a real person: it was a machine. The voice on the machine said, "We are happy to tell you that you now have Internet **access**." But when I went back to my computer, I still couldn't connect to the Internet. I was **furious**!

3   To make a long story short[3], it took the phone company two weeks to solve my problem. I spent a total of 18 hours at home waiting for workers who never came. I spent eight hours on the phone listening to recordings and machines and waiting on hold. Companies think that these voice-activated systems save us time, but they actually waste it.

[1] **DSL:** a fast Internet connection through telephone lines. The letters stand for digital subscriber line.
[2] **technician:** person who fixes machines
[3] **to make a long story short:** to tell something quickly

4   The telephone isn't the only timesaving technology that drives me crazy[4]. The other day, I went to the supermarket. They had a new self-service checkout system. With this new device, I could **scan** my groceries myself instead of waiting in a checkout line. For some strange reason, these machines seem to hate me. Here's what happened:

5   I scan my item. The computer sits there stupidly and does nothing. **Eventually** it says, "Scan your first item." But I already did! What do I do now? Scan it again and get charged twice? So I put my item in the bag.

6   "Put the item in the bag," says the machine. But I already have!

7   "Put the item in the bag," it says again. So, I take it out and do it again, just to make the machine happy.

8   "Scan the item before putting it in the bag!" shouts the machine while everyone turns to look at me as if I'm an idiot[5]. Grrr!

9   I wish we could go back to the good old days when there were real people to help us. I think I would have been happier living a hundred years ago, before we had all of this timesaving, self-service technology.

---

[4] **drive me crazy:** to make me upset or angry
[5] **as if I'm an idiot:** as if they think that I am stupid

MAIN IDEAS

Answer these questions.

1. Why does the writer hate machines?

   _____

2. How did she feel when she used the self-service checkout? Why?

   _____

DETAILS

A. Read the statements. Write _T_ (true) or _F_ (false). Then correct each false statement to make it true.

_____ 1. A worker went to the woman's house to install a phone line.

_____ 2. When the woman called the telephone company, she never got to talk to a real person.

_____ 3. It took the phone company three weeks to solve her problem.

_____ 4. The computer at the supermarket did not work correctly.

_____ 5. The woman thinks she would prefer to have lived in a time before there was technology.

B. Look at Reading 2. Identify who said each of the statements. Write _P_ if it was a person. Write _M_ if it was a computer or an automated voice.

_____ 1. "Remember, you can use our convenient website to solve most of your problems."

_____ 2. "Arrrrrghh!!"

_____ 3. "Why do you think I'm calling you?"

_____ 4. "We're sorry, all agents are busy assisting other customers."

_____ 5. "Scan the item before putting it in the bag!"

 ## WHAT DO YOU THINK?

A. Discuss the questions in a group.

1. Have you ever been frustrated by technology? Describe what happened.

2. Do you prefer to interact with people or with self-service machines? Why?

B. Think about both Reading 1 and Reading 2 as you discuss the questions. Then choose one question and write five to eight sentences in response.

1. Think of a new type of self-service technology. What are the benefits of this technology? What are the disadvantages or problems?

2. How do you think self-service technology could be improved so that people don't get frustrated?

Words with more than one meaning

Many words have more than one meaning, or definition, even if they are spelled and pronounced the same way. Using a dictionary can help you identify the correct meaning of a new word. If a word has two definitions that are the same part of speech (*noun*, *verb*, *adjective*, *adverb*), they will appear under the same entry in the dictionary. If the two meanings are different parts of speech, they will appear under different entries in the dictionary.

---

light¹ 🔑 /laɪt/ *noun* **1** [C, U] the energy from the sun, a lamp, etc. that allows you to see things: *a beam/ray of light* ◆ *the light of the sun* ◆ *The light was too bad for us to read by.* **2** [C] something that produces light, for example an electric lamp: *Suddenly, all the lights came on/went out.* ◆ *the lights of the city in the distance* ◆ *a neon light* ◆ *That car's lights aren't on.* ◆ *Please switch the lights off before you leave.*

light² 🔑 /laɪt/ *adj.*
> **NOT DARK 1** having a lot of light: *In the summer it's still light at 9 o'clock.* ◆ *a light room* **ANT dark**
> **OF A COLOR 2** pale in color: *a light blue sweater* **ANT dark**
> **NOT HEAVY 3** not of great weight: *Carry this bag – it's the lightest.* ◆ *I've lost weight – I'm five pounds lighter than I used to be.* ◆ *light clothes* (= for summer) **ANT heavy**

You can improve your vocabulary by using a dictionary to look up words with more than one meaning.

All dictionary entries are from the *Oxford American Dictionary for learners of English* © Oxford University Press 2011.

A. Use your dictionary to find the different definitions of the words below. Then write the definition and the sentence that uses the word in context. Compare your answers with a partner.

1. row

   Definition 1: _to move a boat through water using long wooden poles with_

   flat ends

   Sentence: _I like to watch the teams row on the river._

   Definition 2: _a line of people or things_

   Sentence: _All of the students lined up in a row._

2. light

   Definition 1: _____

   Sentence: _____

   Definition 2: _____

   Sentence: _____

Definition 3: _____

Sentence: _____

Definition 4: _____

Sentence: _____

3. tip

Definition 1: _____

Sentence: _____

Definition 2: _____

Sentence: _____

Definition 3: _____

Sentence: _____

4. bank

Definition 1: _____

Sentence: _____

Definition 2: _____

Sentence: _____

Definition 3: _____

Sentence: _____

Tip for Success

Sometimes words with more than one meaning are spelled the same way, but they are pronounced differently.

B. Work with a partner. Look up the words *record* and *wind* in the dictionary. Answer the questions below.

1. How many definitions are there for the word *record*? ____

2. How many of the definitions did you already know? ____

3. How many definitions are there for the word *wind*? ____

4. How many of the definitions did you already know? ____

WRITING

When you write about a **process**, you describe how to do something step-by-step. First, you write a topic sentence that states what the process is. Then you explain each step clearly. Use **time order** words to help guide your reader. Time order words usually come at the beginning of a sentence and are followed by a comma. Note that *then* is not followed by a comma.

first	next	then	later	after that	finally

> **First,** turn on your computer.
> **Then** go to our website.

Use these time order words to link two steps in a process.

when	while	as soon as	before	after

> **Before** you download the program, read the directions.
> **While** the program is downloading, you can check your email.

Tip for Success

Use several different time order words in your writing. This will help make your writing more interesting to the reader.

A. Read the instructions for digital dining. Underline the time order words.

Digital dining is an easy way to order food. First, view the menu on your tabletop monitor. Then insert your credit card. Next, use the touch screen to enter your order. When you're ready, push the button to send your order. While you wait for your food, you can take photos and send them to your friends. Finally, use the monitor to pay your bill with a credit card.

B. Read the steps about how to use an ATM card. Then number the steps to show the correct order.

____ a. Press *withdraw.*

____ b. Insert your ATM card.

____ c. Push *done.*

____ d. Read the choices.

____ e. Remove the money from the slot.

____ f. Enter your PIN (*personal identification number*).

____ g. Enter the amount of money.

____ h. Take your receipt and your card.

C. Write the process from Activity B in a paragraph in your notebook, using time order words. You may combine two steps into one sentence.

An **infinitive** is *to* + the base form of a verb. We sometimes use infinitives to show the purpose of an action. **We call these infinitives of purpose.** An **infinitive of purpose** is usually separated from the main verb in a sentence. Infinitives of purpose can be used with most action verbs.

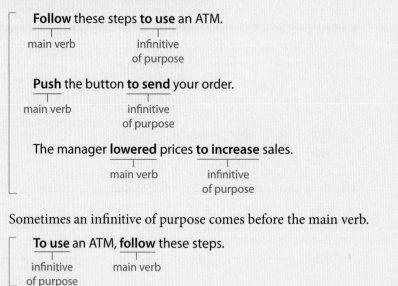

Follow these steps **to use** an ATM.
main verb | infinitive of purpose

Push the button **to send** your order.
main verb | infinitive of purpose

The manager **lowered** prices **to increase** sales.
main verb | infinitive of purpose

Sometimes an infinitive of purpose comes before the main verb.

To use an ATM, **follow** these steps.
infinitive of purpose | main verb

Not all infinitives are infinitives of purpose. An infinitive of purpose has the same meaning as "in order to." If you insert the phrase "in order to," it will help you figure out if an infinitive is one that shows purpose.

Infinitive of purpose:

He called me **to apologize.**
He called me **in order to apologize.** (same meaning)

Not an infinitive of purpose:

He called me and said that he wanted **to apologize.**
He called me and said that he wanted **in order to apologize.** (not the same meaning and incorrect)

A. Underline each infinitive of purpose in the paragraph. Remember, not every infinitive shows purpose.

I make lemonade for my own enjoyment, even though it's easy to buy it at the store. First, I get six lemons to make lemonade. Then I cut the lemons in half and squeeze out the juice. I pour the juice through a strainer to take out the seeds. Next, I add about a half a cup of sugar to a cup of hot water to dissolve the sugar. Finally, I mix the lemon juice, sugar water, and several more cups of water in a pitcher. I add lots of ice to make it cold. It's delicious, and it's my family's favorite summer drink.

B. Answer these questions using infinitives of purpose.

1. Why do you use the Internet?

   _____

2. What is another kind of technology that you use? Why do you use it?

   _____

3. Why do companies use voice-automated telephone systems?

   _____

4. Why are you studying English?

   _____

Unit Assignment | Write a paragraph describing a process

 In this assignment, you are going to write a paragraph describing a process done by a person or a machine. As you prepare to write about a process, think about the Unit Question, "Do you prefer to get help from a person or a machine?" and refer to the Self-Assessment checklist on page 120.

For alternative unit assignments, see the *Q: Skills for Success Teacher's Handbook*.

PLAN AND WRITE

A. **BRAINSTORM** Use the chart to brainstorm ideas for a topic. Then share your ideas with a partner. Decide which topics are the most interesting.

Self-service technology and machines	Things I can make by myself	Things I can repair by myself

Tip Critical Thinking

In Activity B you **identify** the steps in a process. To describe a process, you have to break the process down into separate steps. **Identifying** the steps or parts of a process helps you to understand it better.

B. **PLAN** Complete these activities.

1. Look at your chart in A and select a topic for your paragraph.

2. Think about how you will explain the steps of the process. In your notebook, write the steps in order. Then make a list of time order words you can use to connect the steps of your process.

C. WRITE Write a topic sentence for your paragraph in your notebook. Then use your notes from Activity B to write your paragraph. Use time order words from the Writing Skill on page 117. Use infinitives of purpose where you can. Look at the Self-Assessment checklist below to guide your writing.

REVISE AND EDIT

A. PEER REVIEW Read a partner's paragraph. Answer the questions and discuss them with your partner.

1. Does the topic sentence tell you what the paragraph will be about?

2. How many steps are there? Put a check (✓) at the beginning of each step.

3. Is the process easy to understand? If something is not clear, put a question mark (?) in the margin.

4. Did your partner use time order words and connectors? Circle them.

5. What did you learn by reading the paragraph? What was interesting to you? Write a positive comment about your partner's writing.

B. REWRITE Review the answers to the questions in Activity A. You may want to revise and rewrite your paragraph.

C. EDIT Complete the Self-Assessment checklist as you prepare to write the final draft of your paragraph. Be prepared to hand in your work or discuss it in class.

SELF-ASSESSMENT		
Yes	No	
☐	☐	Is the first line of the paragraph indented?
☐	☐	Does each sentence start with a capital letter and end with a period or question mark?
☐	☐	Is each word spelled correctly? Check a dictionary if you are not sure.
☐	☐	Is there vocabulary from the unit in the paragraph?
☐	☐	Are there any infinitives of purpose?

Circle the words you learned in this unit.

Nouns

access 🔑 AWL

benefit 🔑 AWL

connection 🔑

error 🔑 AWL

Verbs

assist 🔑 AWL

blame 🔑

decrease 🔑

estimate 🔑 AWL

install 🔑

interact AWL

provide 🔑

scan

transfer 🔑 AWL

Adjectives

frustrated

furious

stressed 🔑 AWL

unique 🔑 AWL

Adverbs

automatically 🔑 AWL

eventually 🔑 AWL

Phrases

on hold

🔑 Oxford 3000™ words

AWL Academic Word List

Check (✓) the skills you learned. If you need more work on a skill, refer to the page(s) in parentheses.

READING	○	I can identify the author's purpose. (p. 109)
VOCABULARY	○	I can use the dictionary to identify the correct meanings of words. (p. 115)
WRITING	○	I can describe a step-by-step process. (p. 117)
GRAMMAR	○	I can use infinitives of purpose correctly. (p. 118)
LEARNING OUTCOME	○	I can describe the steps of a process performed by either a person or a machine.

UNIT **7**

Buy or Reuse

READING ● identifying fact and opinion
VOCABULARY ● phrasal verbs
WRITING ● using sentence variety
GRAMMAR ● future time clauses

Unit QUESTION

Is it better to save what you have or buy new things?

PREVIEW THE UNIT

(A) Discuss these questions with your classmates.

What are some things people have repaired? (for example: computers, clothings, watches, cars)

What is the oldest piece of clothing that you still wear? How old is it? Why do you still have it?

Look at the photo. What is the man doing?

(B) Discuss the Unit Question above with your classmates.

Listen to *The Q Classroom*, Track 5 on CD 2, to hear other answers.

123

C Look at the quiz below. Answer the questions about garbage.

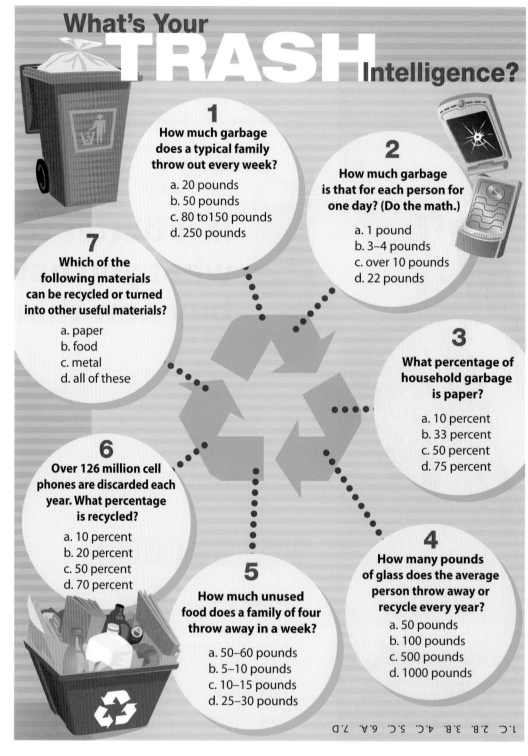

What's Your TRASH Intelligence?

1
How much garbage does a typical family throw out every week?
a. 20 pounds
b. 50 pounds
c. 80 to150 pounds
d. 250 pounds

2
How much garbage is that for each person for one day? (Do the math.)
a. 1 pound
b. 3–4 pounds
c. over 10 pounds
d. 22 pounds

7
Which of the following materials can be recycled or turned into other useful materials?
a. paper
b. food
c. metal
d. all of these

3
What percentage of household garbage is paper?
a. 10 percent
b. 33 percent
c. 50 percent
d. 75 percent

6
Over 126 million cell phones are discarded each year. What percentage is recycled?
a. 10 percent
b. 20 percent
c. 50 percent
d. 70 percent

5
How much unused food does a family of four throw away in a week?
a. 50–60 pounds
b. 5–10 pounds
c. 10–15 pounds
d. 25–30 pounds

4
How many pounds of glass does the average person throw away or recycle every year?
a. 50 pounds
b. 100 pounds
c. 500 pounds
d. 1000 pounds

1.C, 2.B, 3.B, 4.C, 5.C, 6.A, 7.D

D Discuss your answers with a partner. Then look at the answers at the bottom of the quiz. How many did you get correct? Did any answers surprise you?

READING 1 | Think Before You Toss

VOCABULARY

Here are some words from Reading 1. Read their definitions. Then complete each sentence.

> **attitude** (*n*.) the way you think, feel, or behave
> **consequences** (*n*.) things that follow as a result or effect of something else
> **consumer** (*n*.) a person who buys things or uses services
> **disposable** (*adj*.) something you can throw away
> **factor** (*n*.) one of the things that influences a decision or situation
> **feature** (*n*.) an important or noticeable part of something
> **habit** (*n*.) something that somebody does very often
> **persuade** (*v*). to cause somebody to do something by giving him or her good reason
> **possession** (*n*.) something that you have or own

1. Polluting the environment has serious _____ for our
   society. For example, scientists say that air pollution can result in many
   health problems.

2. Miguelina's favorite _____ is the gold necklace her
   grandmother gave her.

3. Eating junk food is a bad _____. It's very unhealthy!

4. There are fewer people shopping in the mall this year than there were last
   year. The average _____ is spending less than last year.

5. My brother worked hard to _____ me to recycle more of my
   trash. I thought it would be too much trouble, but I changed my mind.

6. My printer has a new _____ I really like. It can scan
   photos and print them.

7. Sandra has a very positive _____. She always has a
   cheerful outlook.

8. I can't decide which new car to buy, but the main _____ in my decision will be the price.

9. For the party, we used _____ glasses and plates. We didn't want to wash dishes after the party, so we threw them away.

PREVIEW READING 1

This is a magazine article about the growing problem of too much trash. It discusses some of the reasons for this and suggests some possible solutions.

The author uses the term "throwaway society." What do you think "throwaway society" means?

☐ It's a society that recycles a lot.
☐ It's a society that throws away a lot.
☐ It's a society that isn't important.

 CD 2 Track 6   **Read the magazine article.**

Think Before You Toss

"Why don't you just take them to the shoe repairman? He'll put new soles[1] on, shine them up, and they'll be good for many more years," my grandfather suggested. I was complaining that my favorite shoes were falling apart after only six months.

"Grandpa, that shoe repairman went out of business years ago. No one repairs shoes anymore. And really, I don't mind. I'd rather buy a new pair of shoes, even if they don't last[2] that long."

"Nothing's built to last anymore," he sighed.

1   Perhaps Grandpa has a point[3]. In our modern world, when something wears out, we throw it away and buy a replacement. If a shirt is torn or a coffee machine breaks, you throw it away. The problem is that countries around the world have growing mountains of trash because people are throwing out more trash than ever before. For example, in the United States, the amount of trash per person nearly doubled from 1960 to 2000.

2   How did we become a throwaway society? First of all, it is now easier to replace an item

---

[1] **soles:** the part of the shoe that covers the bottom
[2] **last:** to remain in good condition
[3] **have a point:** to have an important comment in a discussion

than to spend time and money to repair it. Thanks to modern manufacturing and technology, companies are able to produce items quickly and inexpensively. Products are plentiful and prices are low, so we would rather buy something new than repair it. Even if we did want to repair something, many items—from toasters to TVs—are almost impossible to repair. These products contain many tiny, complicated parts. Some even contain small computer chips. It's easier to throw these items away and buy new ones than to fix them.

3   Another contributing **factor** is our love of **disposable** products. As busy people, we are always looking for ways to save time and make our lives easier. Why should we use cloth kitchen towels? It is easier to use a paper towel once and toss it out. Companies manufacture thousands of different kinds of disposable items: paper plates, plastic cups, cameras, and razors for shaving, to name a few. Because these products aren't designed to last, companies know that **consumers** will have to replace them, buying them over and over again. "What's wrong with that?" you ask. The problem is that disposable products are contributing to our trash problem.

4   Our appetite for new products also contributes to the problem. We are addicted to[4] buying new things. As consumers, we want the latest clothes, the best TVs, and cell phones with the newest **features**. Companies tell us to buy, buy, and buy. Advertisements **persuade** us that newer is better and that we will be happier with the latest products. The result is that we throw away useful **possessions** to make room for new ones. In the U.S., when consumers get rid of electronics, 80 percent of them go to a dump. Only about 18 percent of electronics are recycled.

5   All around the world, we can see the **consequences** of this throwaway lifestyle. Dumpsites are mountains of garbage that just keep getting bigger. To lessen the amount of trash and to protect the environment, more governments are requiring people to recycle materials such as paper, plastic, and glass. However, only a small portion of what can be recycled is actually recycled. For example, in the United Kingdom, although about 60 percent of a household's trash can be recycled, only 18 percent actually is. Even though recycling helps, it's not enough to solve our problem of too much trash.

6   Maybe there is another solution. First, we need to repair our possessions instead of throwing them away. As consumers, we should think about how to fix something to make it last. Furthermore, we need to rethink our **attitudes** about spending. Do we really need the latest clothing styles when our closets are full of clothes? Repairing our possessions and changing our spending **habits** may be the best way to reduce the amount of trash and take care of our environment.

What can you do to waste less?	
Think before you buy.	Sell it.
Fix it or get it repaired.	Give it away.
Recycle.	

[4] **addicted to:** unable to stop

MAIN IDEAS

Answer these questions.

1. The author says that we are a throwaway society. What does that mean?

   _____

2. What are four reasons why we throw things away?

   _____

   _____

3. Why do consumers like disposable products?

   _____

4. The author gives her opinion in the last paragraph. What is it?

   _____

DETAILS

Answer these questions.

1. What examples does the author give of products that we usually don't repair?

   _____

2. What examples does the author give of disposable items?

   _____

3. Why do consumers often get rid of useful possessions?

   _____

4. What do these numbers refer to in the article?

   a. 1960–2000: _____

   b. 80 percent, 18 percent: _____

   c. 60 percent, 18 percent: _____

WHAT DO YOU THINK?

Discuss the questions in a group. Then choose one question and write five to eight sentences in response.

1. What items (clothing, electronics, sports equipment) have you recently thrown away? Could the items be repaired? Why or why not? Did you replace them with something new?

2. Think of something that is still useful, but that you no longer want. What can you do with that item instead of throwing it away?

3. Do you think recycling is important? What kinds of things do you recycle?

| Reading Skill | Identifying fact and opinion | |

A **fact** is something that people generally agree is true. Facts are sometimes supported by statistics or other numbers.

> Water freezes at 0° Celsius.
> Paper is one of the easiest materials to recycle.
> In the United States, 18 percent of old TVs are recycled.

An **opinion** is what a person thinks about something. Another person may not agree.

> English is an easy language to learn.
> Consumers are more interested in a product's price than in its quality.
> Advertising has a bad influence on our spending habits.

When reading, it's helpful to understand the difference between facts and opinions. Some words that can indicate an opinion are: (*not*) *think*, (*not*) *believe*, (*not*) *feel*, and in *my opinion*.

> I **don't think** English is an easy language to learn.
> The author **believes** advertising has a bad influence on our spending habits.

A. Read the sentences from Reading 1. Write *F* (fact) or *O* (opinion). Then compare your answers with a partner.

_____ 1. It is now easier to replace an item than to repair it.

_____ 2. Many materials such as paper, plastic, and glass can be recycled, but only a small percentage is actually recycled.

_____ 3. Perhaps recycling is not the answer.

_____ 4. We should think about repairing something before we toss it in the trash.

_____ 5. We are all responsible for taking care of our environment.

_____ 6. People are throwing away twice as much trash as they did 40 years ago.

B. Write a sentence with an opinion and a fact about each topic. Use (*not*) *think*, (*not*) *believe*, (*not*) *feel*, or *in my opinion*.

1. color

    Fact: _Colors can affect how people feel._

    Opinion: _I think pink is a beautiful color._

2. cell phones

    Fact: _____

    Opinion: _____

3. recycling plastic, paper, and glass

    Fact: _____

    Opinion: _____

4. shopping online

    Fact: _____

    Opinion: _____

READING 2 | In Praise of the Throwaway Society

VOCABULARY

Here are some words from Reading 2. Read the sentences. Then write each bold word next to the correct definition.

1. I've never heard the **term** "throwaway society." What does it mean?

2. Sun Joon is a very **materialistic** person. She seems more interested in shopping than making friends.

3. Paul's old jacket is **patched** on the elbows where it used to be ripped.

4. If there's a **significant** amount of snow, the schools will close.

5. Do you think that life forms **exist** in outer space?

6. New flowers in the garden are a **sign** that spring is here.

7. My old cell phone works pretty well, but I really want to get a new **model**.

8. After the soccer game, Khalid put on a **fresh** shirt and put his dirty one in the wash.

9. Kevin and Tanya made a **budget** for March, but they spent more than they planned.

10. Yuki thought that the new phone would cost $50, but the **actual** cost was higher.

a. _____ (*n.*) a plan of how much money you will have and how you will spend it

b. _____ (*adj.*) to be real; to live

c. _____ (*adj.*) clean or new

d. _____ (*adj.*) believing that money and possessions are the most important things in life

e. _____ (*n.*) a certain style of an item that a company makes

f. _____ (*adj.*) covered with cloth to repair a hole

g. _____ (*n.*) something that shows that something exists, is happening, or may happen in the future

h. _____ (*adj.*) important or large enough to be noticed

i. _____ (*n.*) a word or group of words

j. _____ (*adj.*) that really happened; real

**for Success**

Remember that in online posts, people often use informal language. For example, they may use informal words and phrases.

stuff = things

They may also begin sentences with *But* and *And*.

PREVIEW READING 2

You are going to read a blog. In the blog a man gives his opinion about a throwaway society. His opinion is different from the opinion given in Reading 1.

What do you think he will say about a throwaway society?

☐ In a throwaway society, no one should recycle.

☐ A throwaway society shows that people are doing well.

☐ Wealthy people shouldn't throw anything away.

 CD 2
Track 7 · **Read the blog.**

Opinions and thoughts on politics, technology, life, and other stuff.

In praise of the throwaway society

FEBRUARY 26, 2010

Home

Log in

About

Links

Archives

January

February

March

April

May

June

July

August

September

October

November

December

1   Yesterday, I heard someone use the phrase "throwaway society," which got me thinking. Usually, the **term** "throwaway society" is used as a way of saying that we are too **materialistic**. It means that too much of our stuff today is of poor quality instead of being built to last.

2   I see things the opposite way. The fact that we live in a throwaway society isn't a **sign** that things are worse than they used to be. It is a sign that things are better than they have ever been. True, we don't repair things as much as we used to. But that's because we don't have to and don't want to, not because we can't. And it's better that way.

3   I say this because being able to replace instead of repair shows that people are wealthy. What would you rather have: an old repaired laptop or the latest **model**? A pair of socks with the hole **patched** or a **fresh** pair? Some people think that products today are less dependable than they used to be. But most people would rather have something with a newer design, and they vote with their wallets[1].

4   I think there are three reasons for this. First, lower prices. Today, because of technology, it costs less to make items, so they sell for less. When the price difference is small or when it costs more to fix an item than to replace it, consumers naturally decide to pick up a new one. Second, increased wealth. People have more money than they did in the past, and

---

[1] **vote with their wallets:** show their opinion by buying what they want

because of lower prices, they can afford more things. A hundred years ago, most people had one or two sets of clothes. Those clothes were valuable and expensive and formed a **significant** part of their **budget**. Now, you can get a nice sweater for a few dollars. It isn't expensive at all. When that sweater gets a hole in it, you toss it and buy a new one because you can afford to.

5   Third, increased features. Thanks to advances in technology, products are getting better all the time, especially electronics. There is a good chance that the latest model includes some cool features that didn't **exist** when your old one was made. Now, you can get a high-definition[2] digital camera that is small enough to fit in your hand. You can get cell phones that have everything from email to video to GPS[3]. In fact, I hardly ever use my phone for an **actual** phone call anymore because it can do so many other wonderful things. You see, the benefit of increased features is another reason to buy something new. So throw something out today! The throwaway society shows us how good things are.

About Me

Who am I? I am a 28-year-old living in Baltimore, Maryland, in the United States. I grew up in New Jersey, but I went to college in Baltimore and stayed. Now I work at that college in a tech support position. My hobbies include blogging, fooling around[4] with computers, sleeping, selling stuff online, and yelling at the TV.

[2] **high definition:** very good quality
[3] **GPS:** digital tool that can tell you your location
[4] **fool around:** not take something seriously; play or experiment with something

MAIN IDEAS

Circle the answer that best completes each statement.

1. According to Mad Anthony, the throwaway society is a sign that…
   a. we are too materialistic.
   b. things are worse than they have ever been.
   c. things are better than they used to be.

2. Mad Anthony says that…
   a. people would rather have something new.
   b. we can't repair things as easily as before.
   c. replacing instead of repairing is a sign of a weak society.

3. The author of this reading thinks that people should…
   a. fix items rather than replace them.
   b. take pictures with their cell phones.
   c. throw things away when they're old.

DETAILS

With a partner, complete each sentence with information from Reading 2 in your own words. Then look at Reading 2 to check your answers.

1. Today, because of technology, it costs _____ to make items, and so they sell for _____.

2. When the price difference is _____ or when it costs _____ to fix an item than to _____ it, consumers naturally decide to pick up a new one.

3. People have _____ money than they did in the past, and because of _____ prices, they can _____ more things.

4. Thanks to advances in technology, products are getting _____ all the time.

5. The _____ of increased features is another _____ to buy something new.

 WHAT DO YOU THINK?

A. Discuss the questions in a group.

1. What are some of the advantages of buying new things instead of fixing old things? Discuss different items and the advantages of buying the items new.

2. Mad Anthony gives reasons to support his opinion that the throwaway society is a good thing. Do you think these are good reasons? Why or why not?

B. Think about both Reading 1 and Reading 2 as you discuss the questions. Then choose one question and write five to eight sentences in response.

1. Do you think it is better to save and wear old clothing or to buy new, trendy clothes? Why?

2. What kinds of things do you throw away? What habits could you change to throw away less? Can you think of new ways to use these things?

Vocabulary Skill   Phrasal verbs

A **phrasal verb** is a *verb* + a *particle*. Some examples of particles are *in*, *out*, *up*, *over*, *by*, *down*, and *away*. When a particle is added to a verb, it often creates a new meaning.

> I want to **watch** the game on TV tonight.   (watch = look at)
> **Watch out** for ice on the stairs!   (watch out = be careful)

Many phrasal verbs have more than one meaning.

> He **picked up** the book and started to read.   (lifted)
> Beth **picked up** her friend in her new red car.   (gave a ride to)
> The wind **picked up** in the afternoon.   (increased)

Some phrasal verbs are **separable**. They can be separated by objects.

> He **picked up** the book.
> He **picked** the book **up**.
> Yolanda **threw away** her old shoes.
> Yolanda **threw** her old shoes **away**.

Some phrasal verbs are **inseparable**. They cannot be separated by an object.

> ✓ Ollie **fell down** the stairs.
> ✗ Ollie **fell** the stairs **down**.

> ✓ Eva **stopped by** my house yesterday
> ✗ Eva **stopped** my house **by** yesterday.

A. Read the sentences. Then circle the answer that best matches the meaning of each bold phrasal verb.

1. I **wore out** my favorite jeans, so I bought a new pair.
   a. repaired   b. used too much

2. Don't **throw out** the newspaper. I want to read the sports page.
   a. put in the trash   b. put on the floor

3. It's raining, so I'm going to **put on** my raincoat.
   a. wash   b. wear

4. You shouldn't **throw away** plastic bottles. You should recycle them.
   a. reuse   b. put in the trash

5. The shoes at that store are very cheap, but they are not good quality, so they **fall apart** easily.
   a. look nice   b. break into pieces

B. Use each phrasal verb from Activity A in a sentence. Write your sentences in your notebook.

C. Rewrite the sentences putting the object between the verb and particle.

1. We picked up the children from school.

   We picked the children up from school.

2. Please throw away your trash. Don't leave it in the park.

   _____

3. Put on your hat. It's very cold outside!

   _____

4. I'm going to throw out my old watch and buy a new one.

   _____

5. I walk a lot, so I wear out my shoes quickly.

   _____

WRITING

When you use different types of sentences, it makes your writing more interesting to read. When you write, it's important to use different types of sentences. Here are some ways to improve your **sentence variety**.

- Use long and short sentences.
- If you have too many short sentences, combine two sentences into one with a coordinating conjunction (*and*, *but*, *or*, *so*).
- Use questions and imperatives.

Look at these examples from Reading 1.

Perhaps Grandpa has a point. In our modern world, when something wears out, we throw it away and buy a replacement.

Products are plentiful and prices are low, so we would rather buy something new than repair it.

Why should we use cloth kitchen towels? It is easier to use a paper towel once and toss it out.

A. Read this paragraph, and then do items 1–4. Compare your answers with a partner.

    Do you prefer to fix what you have or buy new things? I usually fix the things I have, but I always buy new shoes. I love buying shoes. I already have lots of shoes in different styles and colors, but I always find a new pair that I want to buy. Sometimes after class, I meet my friend Sue. We have coffee, and then we go shopping for shoes at the new shopping center downtown. It's a nice way to spend the afternoon. Are your shoes old and worn out? Don't fix them. Buy a new pair. It's fun!

1. Circle the short sentences in the paragraph.

2. Underline the long sentences in the paragraph.

3. Put a check (✓) next to the questions.

4. Put a star next to the imperatives.

B. Rewrite the paragraph in your notebook and use more sentence variety. You can combine sentences, change sentences, and add more sentences to the paragraph.

Earlier this year, some students noticed that recycling was difficult at our school. There were no containers to collect paper for recycling. People just threw paper away. Also, many students drink bottled water. They throw bottles in the trash without thinking. Student organizers made posters about recycling. They put containers for recycling paper in every classroom and office. In one month, there was a significant increase in the amount of paper in the containers. There were also more bottles in the containers. The organizers are very happy with the results. They hope people's habits continue to change. They hope attitudes change, too.

Grammar | Future time clauses

A **future time clause** is a dependent clause that can be added to a main clause to talk about a future event. Future time clauses begin with a conjunction like *when*, *as soon as*, *after*, *before*, or *not… until*.

> I'll recycle this bottle **when** it is empty.
> I'm going to change my TV **as soon as** I have enough money.
> Mark will take out the garbage **after** he cleans the kitchen.
> I'll let you know **before** I throw those books out. You might want some of them.
> I **won't** buy a new camera **until** this one breaks.

Use *will* or *be going to* in the main clause.

> **I'll paint** the fence before it starts looking old.
> Clovis **isn't going to repair** his computer until the new parts arrive.

Use the simple present in the future time clause. Do not use *will* or *be going to*.

> ✓ I'll help you fix your bike after I **finish** lunch.
> ✗ I'll help you fix your bike after I **will finish** lunch.

Note: The time clause can come first (with a comma) or second (no comma).

> **Before John goes to bed**, he always reads.
> John always reads **before he goes to bed**.

A. Complete each sentence with a future time clause or a main clause. Use the words and phrases in parentheses and the correct punctuation.

1. When I get a new TV, _____ (I/give/my old one/away)

2. _____ (after/Joan/mend/the cover) this couch will look great.

3. I'm not going to sell my car _____ (until/it/break down/again)

4. _____ (as soon as/Jerzy/have/enough time) he is going to buy a new refrigerator.

5. Do you think about what you are doing _____ (before/you/toss/things/in the trash)

6. After Eddie repairs my glasses _____ (they/be/as good as new)

B. Look at the chart. Write five sentences with future time clauses in your notebook. Use one future time clause and one main clause in each sentence. Use the correct form of the verb in parentheses. Punctuate your sentences correctly.

Future time clause	Main clause
When my watch (stop) working	I (call) you
After Sally (finish) her report	she (ask) if her sister wants them
As soon as class (end)	she (go) home
When our car (break) down	we (buy) a new one
Before Patricia (throw) her lecture notes out	I (replace) it

Unit Assignment | **Write a paragraph to answer a test question**

 On some tests, you may have to write one or more paragraphs to answer a question. In this assignment, you are going to write a paragraph to answer the test question, "Is it better to save what you have or buy new things?" As you prepare to write your paragraph, think about the Unit Question and refer to the Self-Assessment checklist on page 140.

For alternative unit assignments, see the *Q: Skills for Success Teacher's Handbook*.

PLAN AND WRITE

A. **BRAINSTORM** Brainstorm ideas about the question in your notebook. Write as many ideas as you can.

B. **PLAN** Make an informal outline to organize your ideas.

It's better to _____

Reason 1: _____

Reason 2: _____

 Tip for Success

In a test situation, you need to quickly organize your ideas before you write your answer. An informal outline is a quick and easy way to plan your writing.

 **Your Writing Process**

For this activity you could also use Stage 1C, *Writing a First Draft* in *Q Online Practice*.

C. WRITE Write a topic sentence for your paragraph in your notebook. Then use your outline from Activity B to complete the paragraph. Include a concluding sentence. Look at the Self-Assessment checklist below to guide your writing.

REVISE AND EDIT

A. PEER REVIEW Read a partner's paragraph. Answer the questions and discuss them with your partner.

1. Does the topic sentence tell you what the paragraph will be about?

2. Does the paragraph answer the question "Is it better to save what you have or buy new things?" Is the writer's opinion clear?

3. Does the paragraph give clear reasons for the opinion? Put a check (✓) next to the reasons.

4. Is there any reference to the readings or to other sources?

5. Did the writer use sentence variety? Did the writer use both short and long sentences? Are there sentences the writer can combine using conjunctions? Put a star (★) next to the future time clauses the writer used.

B. REWRITE Review the answers to the questions in Activity A. You may want to revise and rewrite your paragraph.

C. EDIT Complete the Self-Assessment checklist as you prepare to write the final draft of your paragraph. Be prepared to hand in your work or discuss it in class.

SELF-ASSESSMENT		
Yes	No	
☐	☐	Is the first line of the paragraph indented?
☐	☐	Does each sentence start with a capital letter and end with a period or question mark?
☐	☐	Do the subjects and verbs agree?
☐	☐	Is each word spelled correctly? Check a dictionary if you are not sure.
☐	☐	Is there vocabulary from the unit in the paragraph?
☐	☐	Do you use any phrasal verbs? Are they used correctly?
☐	☐	Are there any future time clauses?

Track Your Success

Circle the words you learned in this unit.

Nouns
attitude 🔑 AWL
budget 🔑
consequence 🔑 AWL
consumer 🔑 AWL
factor 🔑 AWL
feature 🔑 AWL
habit 🔑
model 🔑
possession 🔑
sign 🔑
term 🔑

Verbs
exist 🔑
persuade 🔑

Phrasal Verbs
fall apart
fall down
pick up 🔑
put on 🔑
stop by
throw away 🔑
throw out
watch out
wear out

Adjectives
actual 🔑
disposable AWL
fresh 🔑
materialistic
patched
significant 🔑 AWL

🔑 Oxford 3000™ words
AWL Academic Word List

Check (✓) the skills you learned. If you need more work on a skill, refer to the page(s) in parentheses.

READING ○	I can identify facts and opinions. (p. 129)
VOCABULARY ○	I can use phrasal verbs. (p. 135)
WRITING ○	I can use sentence variety. (p. 137)
GRAMMAR ○	I can use future time clauses. (p. 138)
LEARNING OUTCOME ●	I can respond to a test question by writing a paragraph that states and supports my opinion.

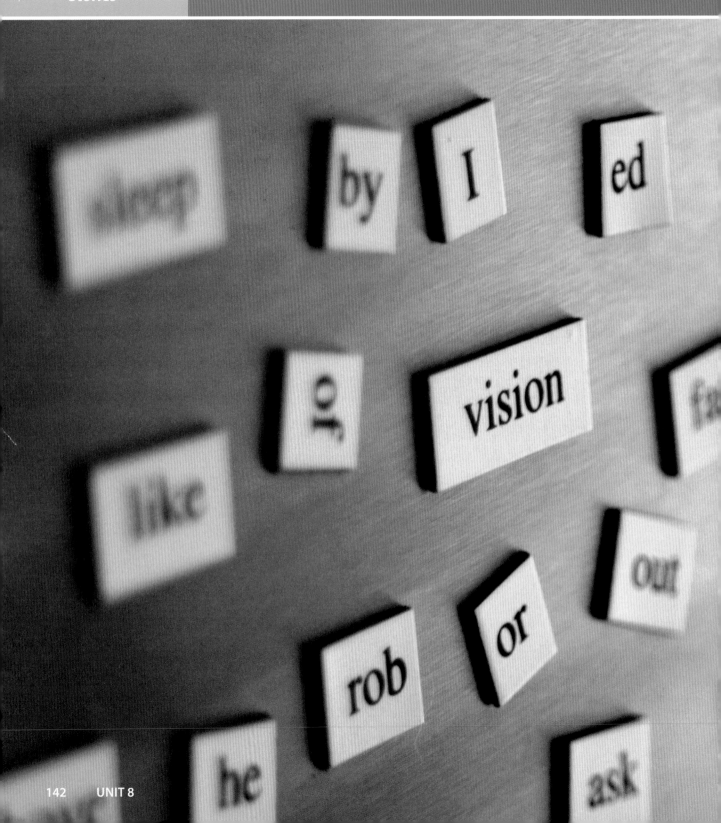

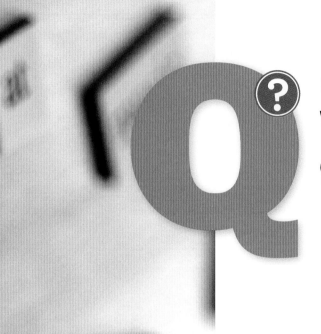

Unit QUESTION

What makes a good story?

PREVIEW THE UNIT

A Discuss these questions with your classmates.

What is your favorite children's story? Why?

Do you feel that you are good at telling stories? Why? Why not?

Look at the photo. What do the words make you think of?

B Discuss the Unit Question above with your classmates.

Listen to *The Q Classroom*, Track 8 on CD 2, to hear other answers.

C Look at the pictures. What different kinds of stories do they represent?
Write the correct word below each picture.

adventure	mystery	folktale	romance

1. _____

2. _____

3. _____

4. _____

D Discuss these questions in a group.

1. Do you know any adventure, mystery, folktale, or romance stories? Which kind is your favorite?

2. What is your favorite kind of story to read? Why?

3. What is your favorite movie? Was it a book first? If so, which is better, the movie or the book? Why?

READING 1 | Nasreddin Hodja and the Candle

VOCABULARY

Here are some words from Reading 1. Read the sentences. Then write each bold word next to the correct definition.

1. Raphael and I made a **bargain**. If I cook, he'll do the dishes.

2. Scientists **challenge** the book that says that global warming isn't real.

3. My parents always **complain** in the winter. They don't like cold weather.

4. Even after I showed him the newspaper article, I couldn't **convince** my brother that the story was true.

5. I really want to go to Hawaii someday. I **imagine** that it's sunny and beautiful.

6. Barry's speeches always **impress** people. They are interesting and creative.

7. Is Jim feeling OK? She isn't acting **normally** today.

8. I enjoy reading about historical events, and I'm **particularly** interested in European history.

9. Angela said that Scott and Mike cheated on the test, but they **protest** their innocence.

10. I **reluctantly** loaned him my car because he's such a fast driver.

a. _____ (*adv.*) in a way that is more than usual

b. _____ (*v.*) to make someone believe something

c. _____ (*adv.*) in a usual or an ordinary way

d. _____ (*adv.*) in a way that shows you don't want to do something because you aren't sure it is right

e. _____ (*n.*) an agreement between people or groups about what each of them will do for the other or others

f. _____ (*v.*) to make someone feel admiration and respect

g. _____ (*v.*) to question whether something is true or right; to argue something is wrong

h. _____ (*v.*) to say something strongly, especially when others do not believe you

Tip for Success

When you visualize something, you picture it in your mind. Visualizing as you read helps you understand the story and remember it.

i. _____ (*v.*) to say that you do not like something or that you are unhappy about something

j. _____ (*v.*) to form a picture or idea of something in the mind

PREVIEW READING 1

This is a Turkish folktale about Nasreddin Hodja. *Hodja* means teacher. The Hodja is a very smart man. In this story, the Hodja's friends challenge him to stay out all night in cold weather without warm clothes. How do you think the Hodja will stay warm?

CD 2
Track 9

Read the folktale.

Nasreddin Hodja and the Candle

1   One day during a **particularly** cold winter, Nasreddin Hodja and his friends sat in a coffeehouse discussing the weather. At first, they spoke **normally**, but soon they were bragging[1] about the things they could do. Before long, the Hodja stuck out his chest proudly: "You may think that we are having a cold winter. Personally, I love the cold and snow. When I was a boy, I used to go out in the middle of January and break the ice on the river so that I could have a good swim in the water. Pooh! This cold is nothing!"

2   His friends did not believe his story. Looking at each other, they decided to **challenge** him. His best friend said, "Hodja, you say that you like cold weather. I suppose you could stay out all night long in the cold without a coat or a blanket or anything at all to warm yourself?"

3   "Of course," said the Hodja.

4   "No fire, no hot tea, no blanket, no coat?" The others seemed **impressed**.

5   "Well," said his friend, "we'll make a **bargain** with you. If you can stay outside tonight, with absolutely nothing extra to warm you all night long, you'll be our guest at a fine dinner. We will pay for everything. Right, friends?"

6   "Right!" they agreed.

7   "On the other hand," his friend continued, "if you use any special item to keep yourself warm, you will have to make dinner for all of us. How about that?"

8   "Fine, fine," agreed the Hodja.

[1] **brag:** to talk too proudly about something

9   That evening the Hodja's friends watched through the windows of their warm houses as the Hodja strolled[2] here and there, studying the stars in the chilly sky and wishing a thousand times that he hadn't agreed to the bargain. It was freezing outside! Just as he was about to give up, he saw a candle in a window about a hundred meters away. Staring thoughtfully at the candle, the Hodja **imagined** that the warmth of the light helped warm the blood flowing through his cold body. By doing this, he was able to stay out all night in the cold.

10   The next morning his friends, stepping outside into the cold air, were amazed to find the Hodja calm and smiling. He seemed to be fine, even though he had stayed outside all night. "Well," said his best friend, "are you sure that you didn't use anything special to warm yourself?"

11   "Not at all," said the Hodja. "Unless you include a candle burning a hundred meters away. I did see a candle, and its burning glow[3] helped me to feel warm during the night. But that doesn't mean that I used anything special. It was just a trick of my mind."

12   "No!" exclaimed his friend. "Hodja, you used that candle to warm yourself. You must be our host at dinner." The Hodja **protested** that he was right and his friends were wrong. Although he tried and tried, he was unable to **convince** them. **Reluctantly** he invited them to dinner at his house that evening.

13   The group arrived in good time and sat on pillows in the living room, waiting for their meal. But they did not smell the delicious smells that would tell them that the Hodja was preparing a fine meal. As time went by, one hour turned into two hours and then into three. The waiting men were hungry and began to **complain**. There was still no food. At last, his friends asked the Hodja about the delay.

14   "Ah, my friends, the dinner is cooking. You can come and see for yourselves," said

the Hodja, and he led them into the kitchen. When they arrived, they were amazed to see a large cooking pot hanging from the ceiling. A single candle was burning one meter below the pot.

15   "But Hodja," said his best friend, "surely you don't expect to heat that pot with a candle. The dinner will never be cooked!"

16   "Oh, I'm not so sure," answered the Hodja, calmly. "If a candle that is a hundred meters away can keep me warm all night long, then surely a candle that is only one meter away can heat a pot for your dinner!"

---

[2] **stroll:** to walk slowly for pleasure
[3] **glow:** a warm light; a look of warmth

MAIN IDEAS

Read the statements. Write *T* (true) or *F* (false). Then correct each false statement to make it true.

_____ 1. The Hodja's friends believed him when he said he loved cold and snow.

_____ 2. The Hodja agreed to stay outside with hot tea and a blanket.

_____ 3. The Hodja imagined that the candle was warming his body.

_____ 4. His friends said that he used a coat to stay warm.

_____ 5. He proved to his friends that the light of a candle could actually warm a person or cook a meal.

DETAILS

Circle the answer that best completes each statement.

1. The Hodja said that when he was young he used to
    a. stay warm all night.
    b. swim in a river in the winter.
    c. do many dangerous things.

2. On the night that the Hodja stayed out,
    a. he stood in one place.
    b. it wasn't as cold as usual.
    c. he wished that he hadn't made the bargain.

3. After the argument in the morning,
    a. the Hodja thought his friends were being unfair.
    b. his friends lost the argument.
    c. the group sat on pillows and waited for the meal.

4. At dinner in the evening,
    a. the Hodja's friends arrived late.
    b. the Hodja's friends enjoyed the food that the Hodja cooked.
    c. the group sat in chairs and waited for the meal.

5. His friends were amazed to see
    a. the Hodja holding the candle.
    b. a single candle below the cooking pot.
    c. the Hodja eating dinner.

 **WHAT DO YOU THINK?**

Discuss the questions in a group. Then choose one question and write five to eight sentences in response.

1. How would you describe Nasreddin Hodja? Is he intelligent? Is he a likable person? Why or why not?

2. The Hodja gets in trouble when he brags to his friends, and he wishes he hadn't made a bargain with them. Why do you think he bragged to them?

3. Do you think this story is trying to teach a lesson? If yes, what do you think the lesson is?

Reading Skill   Summarizing

When you **summarize**, you briefly retell or describe the main ideas or events of a story or an article. Summarizing is a way to check your comprehension and make sure you understand what you've read. Here are some tips for summarizing.

- Take notes about the main ideas and important details as you are reading.
- Put your ideas together into sentences or a paragraph.
- If you have trouble summarizing, go back and reread the parts that you didn't understand.
- If the text is long, you can stop and summarize parts of it at a time.

Here is a summary of the beginning of *Nasreddin Hodja and the Candle*.

> *Nasreddin Hodja and the Candle* is Turkish folktale about a bargain that the Hodja makes with his friends. They are all discussing the cold weather when the Hodja says cold weather doesn't bother him.

 **for Success**

When you summarize, you don't have to use the same tense as the original text. For example, if the story is in the past, you can write the summary in the present.

A. Read Reading 1 again. Take notes about the main ideas and important details for a summary in your notebook.

B. Complete the summary of the first part of Reading 1. Use your notes from Activity A.

The Hodja brags to his friends and _____ them he

_____ . His friends do not believe him, so they make a
   2.

bargain. If he can stay out all night, he'll win and _____ .
                                                          3.

If he can't stay out all night in the cold, his friends will win and he

_____ .
   4.

C. Read the story again. Then with a partner, take turns summarizing the rest of the story aloud.

READING 2 | Writing a Short Story

VOCABULARY

A. Here are some words from Reading 2. Read the sentences. Circle the answer that that best matches the meaning of each bold word.

1. The main **character** in that movie was very funny. He was a wonderful actor.
   a. object in a movie or story
   b. person in a movie or story

2. Tomás was upset yesterday because he had a **conflict** with his father.
   a. argument or problem
   b. meeting

3. No one likes a boring story. A good story is **essential** for the success of a movie.
   a. completely necessary
   b. optional

4. Because Jim doesn't have a job, he is going to **face** many financial problems in the future.
   a. study something
   b. have to deal with something

5. Sarah needs to **overcome** her fear of speaking in front of large groups of people.
   a. control or defeat something
   b. increase or develop something

6. My sister and I need to find a way to **resolve** our disagreements.
   a. find a solution to something
   b. feel angry about something

7. The **setting** for the wedding was a beautiful old country inn.
   a. guests or an event
   b. place where something happens

8. Many movies **take place** in Paris because it's a very beautiful city.
   a. happen
   b. end

9. The novel has a **theme** of family unity, and the story focuses on how the family became closer.
   a. difficult problem
   b. idea that is developed

10. Within a **time span** of five years, Pedro had four different jobs.
    a. limited time
    b. length of time

PREVIEW READING 2

This is a textbook excerpt about writing a short story. It will explain the parts needed for a good story. What parts do you think are needed for a good story?

 CD 2
Track 10 **Read the textbook excerpt.**

Writing a Short Story

1   If your writing assignment is to write a short story, you are probably worried. You might think, "I don't know how to write a story. I don't have a good imagination. I'm not an author!" Believe it or not, writing a short story is easier and more fun than you think. First of all, you already know many stories: personal stories, family stories, stories about your town or country, folktales you heard as a child, and so on. You can write about the funny, surprising, or scary things that have happened to you. Think about the stories that you enjoy telling your friends. Second, this lesson will give you an easy "recipe" for writing your story. This lesson will explain the parts of a story and show you how to write a good short story.

2   American playwright Elmer Rice (1892–1967) said that a play or a story in its simplest form has three parts.

He said that the writer needs to:

1. Put a man up a tree.
2. Throw stones at him.
3. Get him down.

3   This may seem surprisingly simple, but his clever idea works well for many kinds of stories. Let's look at how you can use this recipe for writing your own short story.

1. Put a man up a tree.

4   In part 1, we have two important ingredients of a story: the main **character** and the setting. Your main character is the person at the center of your story. Who is this person? What does your character look like? What is his or her personality? Your **setting** is where your story takes place. This is the physical location of the story. Is the setting on an island? In a house? In some stories, the setting is very important, while in other stories, it isn't. In the example, the setting is a tree, and this is **essential** to the

story. The setting can also include the time of the story. Does it **take place** in the past, the present, or sometime in the future? Also, what is the **time span** of the story? An hour? A day? For a short story, the time span is usually short.

2. Throw stones at him.

5 Part 2 of the story is the **conflict**. The conflict is the problem **facing** the main character. In the example, the character's problem is that he is in a tree, and he wants to come down. There is a conflict between the character and the person who is throwing stones at him. The conflict in a story is the basic problem that your character must **resolve**. What is the problem facing your character? Why is it important? Why does it matter to the main character?

3. Get him down.

6 In part 3, the main character solves the problem or **overcomes** the challenge at the end of the story. He comes down from the tree. This is the resolution of the story. In a good story, the resolution isn't always easy, and the main character may resolve the problem in an unexpected way.

7 By the end of the story, readers understand the **theme** of the story. The theme is the message of the story. What is the story about? What is the reason for the story? Just as the main idea of a paragraph is supported by details, the theme is supported by the setting, the main character, and the conflict.

8 When you write your own short story, keep these three parts in mind. Remember that you are using words to paint a picture for your reader. It's like a movie you have seen, and now you are describing the story to a friend. Does that sound like fun? Well, get started!

MAIN IDEAS

Answer these questions.

1. What is the author's purpose? What is he or she trying to do?

   _____

2. What are the three main parts of a story?

   _____

3. Define *conflict* in your own words.

   _____

4. In which part of the story is the resolution?

   _____

DETAILS

Answer these questions.

1. The writer gives examples of four kinds of stories that you already know. What are they?

   _____

2. Who was Elmer Rice?

   _____

3. Who is the main character?

   _____

4. What is the setting? Give an example.

   _____

5. What is the theme of the story?

   _____

 WHAT DO YOU THINK?

A. Discuss the questions in a group.

1. Do you think that Rice's three-step "recipe" is a good way to write a story? Why or why not?

2. Have you ever written a story? What was it about? Why did you write it?

B. Think about both Reading 1 and Reading 2 as you answer these questions. Then choose question 2 or 3 and write five to eight sentences in response.

1. What is the setting of *Nasreddin Hodja and the Candle*?

   _____

2. The Hodja has two problems, or conflicts in the story: one near the middle of the story and one near the end. Summarize the conflicts and how the Hodja resolves each one.

3. In a good story, the main character "may resolve the problem in an unexpected way." Did the Hodja resolve his problem in an unexpected way? Were you surprised? Why? Why not?

A **connotation** is an impression or feeling that a word gives a person in addition to its literal meaning.

> The candle's **glow** was orange and yellow.
> The candle's **light** was orange and yellow.

Light and *glow* mean similar things. A writer might choose to use *glow* instead of *light* because *glow* gives the reader a stronger impression. It gives the connotation of warmth coming from the light and a feeling of being comfortable.

Sometimes a dictionary can help you figure out the connotation of a word.

light¹ /laɪt/ *noun* **1** [C, U] the energy from the sun, a lamp, etc. that allows you to see things: *a beam/ray of light* ✦ *the light of the sun* ✦ *The light was too bad for us to read by.* **2** [C] something that produces light, for example an electric lamp: *Suddenly, all the lights came on/went out.* ✦ *the lights of the city in the distance* ✦ *a neon light* ✦ *That car's lights*

glow² /gloʊ/ *noun* [sing.] **1** a dull, steady light: *The city was just a red glow on the horizon.* **2** a feeling or look of warmth or satisfaction: *The fresh air had brought a healthy glow to her cheeks.* ✦ *When she looked at her children, she felt a glow of pride.*

Understanding connotations gives you a better understanding of what you read. It can also make your writing more descriptive and interesting.

All dictionary entries are from the *Oxford American Dictionary for learners of English* © Oxford University Press 2011.

Read the pairs of sentences. What is the difference in connotation in the underlined words? Circle the correct answer. Use a dictionary to help you.

1. After she realized her mistake, she was <u>furious</u>.
   After she realized her mistake, she was <u>angry</u>.
   Furious is (stronger than / not as a strong as) *angry.*

2. Ethan is very tall and <u>thin</u>.
   Ethan is very tall and <u>skinny</u>.
   Thin is (more negative / more positive) than *skinny.*

3. I'm <u>tired</u>. I'm going to bed.
   I'm <u>exhausted</u>. I'm going to bed.
   Tired is (stronger than / not as strong as) *exhausted.*

4. There is a <u>smell</u> coming from the kitchen.
   There is an <u>odor</u> coming from the kitchen.
   Smell is more (positive / negative) than *odor.*

5. My sister and I <u>disagreed</u> about which movie to see.
   My sister and I <u>argued</u> about which movie to see.
   Disagreed is (stronger than / not as strong as) *argued.*

WRITING

A **narrative** is a story or a description of an event. The following are important elements in a narrative.

- When you write a narrative, include a description of the **setting**. It should be clear when and where the story occurs.

- Show a clear **sequence** (the order in which things happen). Use time order words to make the story sequence clear to your readers. (See Unit 6, page 117.)

> **After** lunch, I was very sleepy, so I decided to close my eyes.
> **When** I woke up, it was dark outside and everyone was gone.

- Include **sensory details** that describe what your characters *see, hear, feel, smell*, and *taste*. Descriptive words will help the reader visualize and experience the narrative.

> The hot soup **smelled strongly** of pepper and onions, reminding him of home.

A. Read the story. Then circle the words that help to show the sequence of events. Underline the words that show sensory details.

At the beginning of the folktale, Aladdin was only a poor boy dressed in old clothes. When he went into a cave, he found a shiny lamp glowing in the dark. He gently picked it up and rubbed it. Suddenly, a large magical genie appeared. The genie was huge and spoke in a deep voice. The genie explained that Aladdin could have three wishes. After Aladdin left the cave, his life became an exciting adventure. Later, because of his wishes, Aladdin became rich and powerful. Finally, he was able to marry a princess and live in a beautiful palace.

B. Imagine what happened next. Use your own ideas to complete each of the sentences below.

1. When I opened the front door, _____.

2. As soon as the man walked into the room, _____.

3. After my credit card was stolen, _____.

4. Before I jumped into the deep water, _____.

5. When I opened the mysterious letter, _____.

C. Fill in the blanks. Use your imagination to add sensory details. Use descriptive words to help describe the senses in parentheses.

1. (smell) The smell of _____ cake _____ reminded Jonathan of

   ___ his grandmother's kitchen ___ .

2. (hearing) The sound of _____ made Sossi think

   of _____ .

3. (taste) Sam ate the hot soup. It tasted _____ .

   It filled his mind filled with memories of _____ .

4. (sight) When she saw the beautiful _____, Peggy

   thought that it looked like _____ .

5. (feel) When Victoria got into her bed after a long day, it felt

   _____. It made her think of

   _____ .

Grammar | Simple past and past continuous web

Use the **simple past** to describe a single completed action or a series of completed actions in the past.

> I **bought** the new novel by my favorite author yesterday.
> Barbara **drove** home, **unloaded** her car, and **made** a cup of coffee.

Also use the simple past to describe a habitual or repeated action in the past.

> Last summer, I **went** to the movies every weekend.
> I **sent** Shirley three emails, but she never replied.

Use the **past continuous** to emphasize the duration of an action in the past.

> I **was talking** on the phone for hours last night.
> My brother **was acting** strangely last night.

If a past event was interrupted by another event or series of events, use *while* or *when* with the past continuous for the interrupted event. Use the simple past for the event or events that interrupted it.

> Marianne *left* the room **while** the storyteller **was** still **talking**.
> **When** I **was studying** in Korea, I *met* many interesting people.

A. Read the sentences. Check (✓) the use of the past simple in the sentence.

	single action	series of actions	repeated action
1. I **left** the restaurant at 6 p.m. last night.	☐	☐	☐
2. When the president **came** into the room, everyone **stood** up and **clapped**.	☐	☐	☐
3. Eric **rewrote** his story five times.	☐	☐	☐
4. My friend **visited** me every day while I was sick.	☐	☐	☐
5. Someone **stole** my bike last week.	☐	☐	☐
6. Brenda **finished** her letter, **put** it in an envelope, and **took** it to the post office.	☐	☐	☐

B. Read the sentences. Check (✓) the use of the past continuous (in bold) in the sentence.

	duration	interrupted action
1. Jim broke his leg while he **was playing** soccer.	☐	☐
2. I **was watching** TV all weekend.	☐	☐
3. When Michael **was working** in the science lab, he discovered a mistake.	☐	☐
4. You **were complaining** the whole time at the movies last night.	☐	☐

C. Complete the paragraph with the simple past or past continuous.

As soon as I _____ the front door of my apartment,
1. (unlock)

I _____ something was wrong. The TV _____
2. (know)   3. (be)

on, but no one _____ it. Then I _____
4. (watch)   5. (smell)

something burning. I started to worry. While I _____
6. (walk)

toward the kitchen to see what the smell was, I _____
7. (hear)

some noises. Suddenly, about ten of my friends _____ out
8. (jump)

of the kitchen. They all _____, "Surprise!" While they
9. (yell)

_____ "Happy Birthday," I _____ the cake
10. (sing)   11. (take)

out of the oven. After we _____ burnt cake, my friends
12. (eat)

_____ me some presents.
13. (give)

| Unit Assignment | Write a short story |

In this assignment, you are going to write a story (narrative) using the steps you learned in Reading 2. As you prepare your story, think about the Unit Question, "What makes a good story?" and refer to the Self-Assessment checklist on page 160.

For alternative unit assignments, see the *Q: Skills for Success Teacher's Handbook*.

Tip Critical Thinking

In the Unit Assignment, you will **compose** a story. **Composing** is thinking carefully about something before or as you write. Thinking carefully about your ideas will make your writing stronger.

PLAN AND WRITE

A. BRAINSTORM Complete the activities.

1. Brainstorm a list of ideas for your story in your notebook. They can be ideas for a folktale, a personal story, or a story from your imagination.

2. In a group, explain your two best story ideas. Ask your classmates which idea they prefer and why.

B. **PLAN** Choose a story to write, and then answer these questions.

1. Who is the main character? What adjectives describe this person? What details about the person are important for your story?

_____

_____

_____

2. What is the setting? Where does the story take place?

_____

_____

3. When and where does your story begin? When and where does it end?

_____

_____

4. Is there a conflict? What is it? How is it resolved?

_____

5. What sensory details can you include to make the story or narrative seem more real or interesting to the reader?

_____

6. Write the events of your story in order in your notebook.

Tip for Success

If you write dialogues in your stories, be sure to use quotation marks.

"Where are you going?" he asked.

"It's none of your business," I replied.

C. **WRITE** Write your story in your notebook. Use your answers to the questions in Activity B to help you. Look at the Self-Assessment checklist on page 160 to guide your writing.

REVISE AND EDIT

A. **PEER REVIEW** Read a partner's story. Answer the questions and discuss them with your partner.

1. Who is the main character?

2. What is the conflict? Is it clear?

3. What does the character do to resolve the conflict?

4. Is the resolution surprising? Is it a good resolution?

5. What do you like about the story? Talk about two things you like.

6. Did your partner include sensory details? Suggest a few words that could be changed or added to make the story more interesting.

B. **REWRITE** Review the answers to the questions in Activity A. You may want to revise and rewrite your story.

C. **EDIT** Complete the Self-Assessment checklist as you prepare to write the final draft of your story. You may want to rewrite it. Be prepared to hand in your work or discuss it in class.

SELF-ASSESSMENT		
Yes	**No**	
☐	☐	Is the first line of the paragraph indented?
☐	☐	Is each word spelled correctly? Check a dictionary if you are not sure.
☐	☐	Do the subjects and verbs agree?
☐	☐	Is there vocabulary from the unit in the story?
☐	☐	Do you use the simple past? Check to make sure it is correct.
☐	☐	Do you use the past continuous? Check to make sure it is correct.

Track Your Success

Circle the words you learned in this unit.

Nouns
bargain 🔑
character 🔑
conflict 🔑 AWL
setting
theme 🔑 AWL

Verbs
challenge 🔑 AWL
complain 🔑

convince 🔑 AWL
face 🔑
imagine 🔑
impress 🔑
overcome 🔑
protest 🔑
resolve 🔑 AWL

Adjectives
essential 🔑

Adverbs
normally 🔑 AWL
particularly 🔑
reluctantly AWL

Phrasal Verbs
take place 🔑

Phrases
time span

🔑 Oxford 3000™ words
AWL Academic Word List

Check (✓) the skills you learned. If you need more work on a skill, refer to the page(s) in parentheses.

READING	○	I can summarize. (p. 149)
VOCABULARY	○	I can understand connotations. (p. 154)
WRITING	○	I can write a narrative. (p. 155)
GRAMMAR	○	I can use simple past and past continuous. (p. 156)
LEARNING OUTCOME	●	I can write a short story that includes a main character, setting, conflict, and resolution.

READING ● making inferences
VOCABULARY ● numbers and mathematical terms
WRITING ● using numbers to support ideas
GRAMMAR ● the present perfect

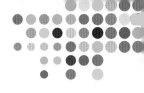

LEARNING OUTCOME

Describe your personal experience of learning math in a paragraph that includes numbers and facts.

Unit QUESTION

Does everyone need math?

PREVIEW THE UNIT

Ⓐ Discuss these questions with your classmates.

Do you like or dislike doing math? Why?

Can you think of any jobs that don't use math?

Look at the photo. How is this person using math?

Ⓑ Discuss the Unit Question above with your classmates.

◉ Listen to *The Q Classroom*, Track 11 on CD 2, to hear other answers.

C Look at the math trivia quiz below. Answer the questions.

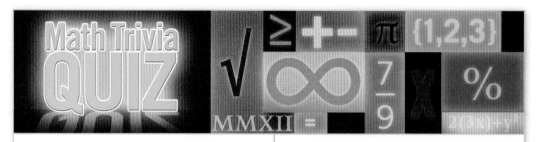

1 What is the mathematical term for a shape with eight equal sides?

   a. a hexagon

   b. a cube

   c. an octagon

2 What two letters both mean 1,000?

   a. L and D

   b. K and M

   c. K and Q

3 In what century did mathematicians first start using plus (+) and minus (–) signs?

   a. the fifteenth century

   b. the sixteenth century

   c. the seventeenth century

4 What number did al-Khwarizmi, an Arab mathematician, give to the West?

   a. zero

   b. googol

   c. π

5 What number does "giga" represent?

   a. one thousand

   b. one million

   c. one billion

6 How do you write 50 in Roman numerals?

   a. C

   b. D

   c. L

7 What Greek mathematician discovered that the morning star and evening (night) star are the same thing?

   a. Euclid

   b. Pythagoras

   c. Plato

8 What number that includes 100 zeros was first used by a nine-year old boy in 1938?

   a. googol

   b. a zillion

   c. infinity

Answers: 1. c. octagon, 2. b. K and M, 3. b. the sixteenth century, 4. b. zero, 5. c. one billion, 6. c. L, 7. b. Pythagoras, 8. a. googol

D Discuss your answers in a group. Then check the answers at the bottom of the page.

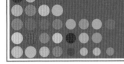
READING 1 | Cultural Differences in Counting

VOCABULARY

Here are some words from Reading 1. Read their definitions. Then complete each sentence.

> **as opposed to** (*prep. phrase*) in contrast with
> **assume** (*v.*) to accept or believe that something is true though you have no proof
> **determine** (*v.*) to find something out
> **extend** (*v.*) to stretch out a part of the body
> **indicate** (*v.*) to be or give a sign about something
> **method** (*n.*) a way of doing something
> **precise** (*adj.*) accurate
> **pick it up** (*v.*) to learn something without formal lessons
> **remote** (*adj.*) far away from where other people live

1. Kathryn's sister taught her a new _____ for making coffee.

2. Joanna told the students in her yoga class to _____ their arms fully.

3. Dr. Adair's long career in science taught him to make _____ measurements.

4. Paul and Shana were tired of the city, so they moved to a _____ place in the countryside.

5. Many people _____ that I speak Spanish because my last name is Gonzales, but I actually only speak English.

6. I never studied Chinese, but I managed to _____ while I was teaching in Hangzhou.

7. It's easy to get along with Jenny, _____ Stephen, who can be pretty difficult.

 **Tip** for Success

Signal words like *in addition* or *for example* usually alert you to important information in a text.

8. After many difficult studies, the researcher was finally able to

_____ the cause of the problem.

9. The baby lifts her arms to _____ that she wants someone to

pick her up.

PREVIEW READING 1

This is a science report that describes some of the ways people think about numbers and math in different parts of the world. It describes the way people count and the language that they use for numbers. Do you think all cultures count in the same way?

 CD 2
Track 12

Read the science report.

Cultural Differences in Counting

1   How quickly can you count from one to ten? Do you use ten different words to do it? Can you do it in English, or do you have to use your first language? Do you count on your fingers? Many people **assume** that numbers and math are the same all over the world. But scientists have discovered that this is not true.

2   People in different parts of the world use different **methods** to count on their fingers. In the United States, people begin counting with their first, or index, finger, which they

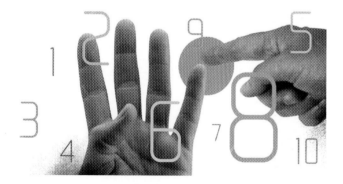

extend or stick out. They then extend the rest of their fingers and finally the thumb to count to five. Then they repeat this with the other hand to get to ten. In some cultures, people begin with their fingers already extended. They count by folding the fingers inward. In China, people count by using a variety of finger positions. In this way, a Chinese person can easily count to ten on only one hand, while an American uses two hands to count to ten.

3   In addition to methods of finger counting, scientists have found that cultures and languages also differ when it comes to numbers. Some languages have only a few words for numbers, and others don't have any words for numbers. A group of scientists worked with aboriginal[1] children in Australia. The scientists studied people who have a very small vocabulary for numbers. Unlike many groups, these people don't have gestures or hand movements to **indicate** numbers. In most cultures, people count on fingers to indicate a number, but not in these aboriginal tribes[2].

---

[1] **aboriginal:** of or belonging to the race of people who were the original inhabitants of Australia

[2] **tribe:** a group of people that have the same language and customs and that are ruled by a chief or chiefs

The Australian scientists found out that even though the children do not have words or gestures for counting, they are still able to understand different ideas about numbers.

4   In tests, aboriginal children listened to taps from a stick and then put out markers to match the number of taps they heard. For example, if they heard four taps, the scientists wanted to see if they put out four markers. They had to connect numbers with sounds and with actions, without seeing written numbers. In the tests, the children put out the correct number of markers. They were able to count even though they didn't have words for numbers. Experts believe this shows that humans have a universal ability to count.

5   In a similar study, researchers from the Massachusetts Institute of Technology traveled to a **remote** location in northwestern Brazil to test members of the Pirahã tribe. The researchers conducted experiments and discovered that the tribespeople don't have words for numbers. They do have words that mean "some" and "more," but they don't have words for **precise** numbers such as "one" or "three." Instead, they express quantities in relative[3] terms—that is, in comparison to other numbers or objects. So a tribesperson is not able to say "five trees" or "ten trees" but can say "some trees," "more trees," or "many trees."

6   Professor Edward Gibson said that most people assume that everyone knows how to count, "but here is a group that does not count. They could learn, but it's not useful in their culture, so they've never **picked it up**."

7   In their everyday lives, the Pirahã appear to have no need for numbers. The scientists

The Pirahã appear to have no need for numbers.

never heard them use words like "all" or "every." There is one word, "hói," which does come close to the number one. But it can also mean "small" or describe a small amount, like two small fish **as opposed to** one big fish. The Pirahã don't even appear to do simple math or even count on their fingers to **determine** how many pieces of meat they need to cook. Because they don't need numbers, their language doesn't include them.

8   Although all humans have the ability to understand quantities, not all languages have numbers and not all people use counting. Number words in a particular language are a result of people needing numbers in their daily lives. Scientists are gaining a new understanding of which abilities (such as counting) are universal and which are learned. Because of the work of these scientists, now we know that people have different ideas about numbers and math, too.

___

[3] **relative:** when compared to something else

MAIN IDEAS

Circle the answer to each question.

1. What do we learn from the difference in finger counting between the United States and China?
   a. People from the U.S. count faster than people from China.
   b. People from China need two hands to count to ten.
   c. People in different parts of the world use different methods to count on their fingers.

2. What was the scientists' main discovery about the aboriginal people in Australia?
   a. Aboriginal people have only a small vocabulary for numbers.
   b. Aboriginal people can understand ideas about numbers even if they don't have words for them.
   c. Children couldn't put out markers that matched the number of sounds.

3. Why did scientists want to study the Pirahã tribe?
   a. The tribespeople didn't have words for numbers.
   b. The tribe lived in a remote area.
   c. The scientists assumed that everyone knows how to count.

4. Why didn't the Pirahã use words for numbers?
   a. They didn't need to use them in daily life.
   b. They did have some words for precise numbers.
   c. People in remote areas generally don't need to know math.

5. What is the main idea of the article?
   a. Chinese people can count more efficiently on their fingers than Americans can.
   b. People from different cultures have different ideas about numbers and math.
   c. In some remote cultures, people don't know how to count.

DETAILS

Read the statements. Write *T* (true) or *F* (false).

_____ 1. People in the United States need to use two hands to count to ten on their fingers.

_____ 2. All languages have words for numbers.

_____ 3. People in the aboriginal tribes in Australia cannot count on their fingers.

_____ 4. In tests, aboriginal children had to match pictures with numbers.

_____ 5. The scientists who went to Brazil were from the California Institute of Technology.

_____ 6. The Pirahã tribe are aboriginal people in Australia.

_____ 7. The Pirahã don't have words for precise numbers.

_____ 8. The tribes in the study live in urban areas.

_____ 9. The Pirahã have a word that can mean "one" or "two."

_____ 10. The Pirahã need to use numbers in their everyday lives.

 ## WHAT DO YOU THINK?

Discuss the questions in a group. Then choose one question and write five to eight sentences in response.

1. What was the most surprising thing that you learned in this article?

2. The Pirahã tribe and the aboriginal people in Australia don't really seem to need numbers. What kinds of things do you use numbers for in your daily life? Can you imagine a day without numbers? Why or why not?

| Reading Skill | Making inferences | |

When you make an **inference** about a text, you determine that something is true even though the writer does not tell you directly.

> Suzy yawned as she tried to keep her eyes open.

You can **infer** that Suzy was tired, even though the writer didn't say, "Suzy was tired." You can infer this because usually when people yawn and can't keep their eyes open, they are tired. However, you can't infer that she stayed up all night. There are no clues in the text to suggest this, and there are many reasons she could be tired.

To make inferences, use clues from the text and your own knowledge and experience to figure out what the author is trying to tell you. Making inferences is a useful skill because it's a way to gain a deeper understanding of the text. It is sometimes called "reading between the lines."

A. Read the sentences. Then circle the inference you can make for each.

1. During their vacation, they didn't have phone service or Internet service.
   a. They were in a remote location.
   b. They didn't have a cell phone.

2. My brother loves to fix cars.
   a. He has a car that he likes to repair.
   b. He's good at repairing mechanical things.

3. When Marcia got home, she walked to her bedroom without speaking to anyone and slammed the door.
   a. She was angry.
   b. She broke the door.

4. Alex always assumed that he would be a doctor.
   a. He wanted to be a doctor for a long time.
   b. He went to medical school.

B. Read the paragraph and the inferences. Write *Y* (yes) if it <u>is</u> an inference you can make, or *N* (no) if it <u>is not</u> an inference you can make.

> The house was completely quiet. The only sounds were the hum of the refrigerator and the tick-tock of the kitchen clock. Rosie's math book and review sheets were on the table in front of her, but she could barely keep her eyes open. She needed to review two more pages before going to bed. She really had to get a good test score tomorrow or she would fail the class.

_____ 1. Rosie was studying at night.

_____ 2. She was sitting at the kitchen table.

_____ 3. Rosie is a teenager.

_____ 4. Rosie is worried about a math test.

_____ 5. Rosie isn't very good at math.

_____ 6. Rosie's family was awake.

C. Read each sentence about Reading 1. Then circle the inference you can make.

1. The Pirahã could learn to count, but it's not useful in their culture, so they've never picked it up.
   a. They probably don't think that counting is important in their lives.
   b. They probably don't count because there is no school where they live.

2. The Pirahã people don't count and don't have words for numbers.
   a. They are not intelligent.
   b. They probably don't use money in their daily lives.

3. The researchers tested aboriginal children in the study.
   a. They tested children because they are easier to work with than adults.
   b. They tested children because adults may have learned how to count.

4. In tests, aboriginal children listened to taps from a stick and then put out markers to match the number of taps they heard.
   a. Aboriginal children have very good hearing.
   b. Researchers gave the children sticks and markers for the test.

READING 2 | Problems with Math

VOCABULARY

Here are some words from Reading 2. Read the sentences. Circle the answer that best matches the meaning of each bold word or phrase.

1. When I saw my five-year-old son wearing my husband's clothes, I couldn't hide my **amusement**.
   a. finding something funny
   b. finding something sad
   c. feeling embarrassed

2. The directions were **complicated**. We had trouble understanding them.
   a. disturbing
   b. difficult
   c. clear

3. Multiplication is a very basic **concept** that is taught in elementary math classes.
   a. idea
   b. book
   c. object

4. I was **flattered** when she told me that she thought I was intelligent.
   a. upset
   b. confused
   c. pleased

5. I couldn't understand her voice message. It didn't **make sense**.
   a. have value
   b. have a clear meaning
   c. translate

6. I often **overestimate** how much time I need to do my homework. I usually finish it more quickly than I expect.
   a. be annoyed with
   b. be sure about
   c. guess too high

7. He studied the entire **process** of manufacturing a car from beginning to end.
   a. series of actions
   b. conclusion
   c. research

8. The best way to choose a good restaurant is to ask someone for a **recommendation**.
   a. discount
   b. suggestion
   c. directions

9. I don't like reading the introductions to books, so I usually **skip** them.
   a. repeat something
   b. add something
   c. leave something out

10. Even though I study a lot, I **struggle** to get good grades.
    a. have a hard time
    b. fight with someone
    c. don't try

PREVIEW READING 2

You are going to read a personal essay in a magazine. The author describes his difficulties with math, both as a child and as an adult. What problems do you think he will describe?

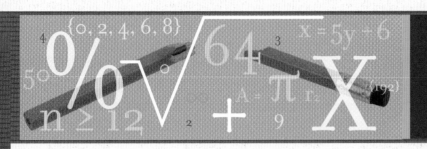

Problems with Math

1   Are you good at math? I'm not. I was pretty good at math at the beginning of elementary school. I didn't have any problems learning addition or subtraction. Multiplication was OK. It was when we got to division in the fourth grade that things began to go downhill[1]. I don't remember very much about math for the next several years. But then I had a serious problem.

2   When I went from junior high school to high school, my math teacher had to make a **recommendation** for what courses I should take. She **overestimated** my math ability, and she had me **skip** some courses that I really should have taken. I managed to squeak by[2] in Algebra[3] 1. Then there was Geometry[4]. I loved this class. Measuring angles and shapes **made sense**

Math teacher Dick Peller

to me. But then I had to take Algebra 2. Here I ran into trouble.

3   Remember all those ideas and **concepts** that I didn't really learn in Algebra 1? Now I needed to depend on those concepts in the Algebra 2 course. But I didn't know them. Even though my teacher gave me extra help, I didn't do very well in that course. Finally, I made it to my last year in high school and took an advanced course in math, Trigonometry[5]. After the course, my teacher, Mr. Peller, sent a note home to my parents along with my grades. "I think it would be better if Joe didn't take any more math," he wrote in the note. I'm sure that he had my best interests at heart[6]. He knew that if my grades were bad, I might have difficulty getting into a good university.

4   Fortunately for me, I did manage to get into college. Many colleges and universities in the United States require students to take courses in a variety of different subject areas, including math and science. I was lucky because my university didn't have such requirements, so I didn't need to take math. Instead, I took a course called The Philosophy of Mathematics. I don't think that I would have taken the class, except that a friend of mine decided to enroll, and she convinced me to enroll, too. The professor was very interesting and was passionate[7] about his

---

[1] **things began to go downhill:** things began to go badly
[2] **squeak by:** to just barely succeed
[3] **Algebra:** a type of math that uses letters and symbols to represent numbers and amounts
[4] **Geometry:** the study of shapes, lines, etc. and the math related to them
[5] **Trigonometry:** the study of relationships between angles and sides of triangles
[6] **he had my best interests at heart:** he wanted what was best for me
[7] **passionate:** felt very strongly

subject. And the class was really more about ideas than about numbers. For instance, one of the questions we discussed was, "Do numbers really exist independently, or are they just an idea that humans invented?" In other words, is "two" really just an idea that people have? If there were no people, would there still be "two"? Guess what? I got an "A" in this course and the next year, Professor Davis asked me if I wanted a job as a teaching assistant[8]. I was **flattered**, but I said, "No, thanks." I was afraid that my poor abilities in math would be discovered.

5 Some years later, I got married. My wife, Leila, is especially good at math. We would sometimes go out to dinner in restaurants. When it came time to pay the bill, I always **struggled** to figure out the correct amount to leave as a tip for the server—usually 15 percent of the total. Leila used to look at me in **amusement**. Finally one night, she said, "Tell me what **process** you go through when you are trying to calculate the tip."

6 I said, "OK. I want to leave a 15 percent tip. So first, I take the total amount of the bill, and then I divide it by 10 in order to figure out 10 percent. Then, I take the amount that is 10 percent, and I divide it by two and that gives me 5 percent. Then, all I have to do is add the amount that is 10 percent to the amount that is 5 percent, and I get 15 percent." I thought I had explained things rather well.

7 She looked at me as if I were a small child. Then she said, very gently, "You know, it's so much easier just to divide by seven." Well, this didn't seem easier for me because, as I said, I found division to be more **complicated**

than addition and subtraction. I thought her method was more difficult. But do you know what? I tried it a few times, and she was right. All you need to do is divide the total by seven, which gives you an estimate, and then you just add a little more. It is really quite easy.

My method

$28.00 (total)
$28.00 ÷ 10 = $2.80 (10% of total)
$2.80 ÷ 2 = $1.40 (5% of total)

$2.80 (10% of total)
+ $1.40 (5% of total)
_____

= $4.20 (15% of total)
($4.20) = tip

Leila's method

$28.00 (total) ÷ 7 = $4.00
($4.00) = tip

8 Now that we have a small child, we don't eat in restaurants very often. But I finally found a good solution to my problems with math: my wife, the math expert. She handles most of our bills, and when our son comes to me and asks me a question about math, all I have to say is, "Ask your mother!"

[8] **teaching assistant:** a more advanced student who helps to teach a class for other students at a university, often shortened to T.A.

MAIN IDEAS

Read the sentences. Then number them in the order that the ideas appear in Reading 2.

_____ a. A teacher overestimated the author's ability at math, so he skipped some important classes.

_____ b. Things began to go downhill with long division.

_____ c. The author lets his wife worry about things that require math.

_____ d. The author didn't have any trouble with math at first.

_____ e. The author studied the philosophy of mathematics.

_____ f. The author learned a new way to calculate tips in restaurants.

_____ g. The author struggled with algebra and trigonometry in high school.

DETAILS

Answer these questions.

1. In what grade did the author's problems with math begin?

_____

2. What math classes did he take in high school?

_____

3. Why didn't the author want to be a teaching assistant?

_____

4. What is the advantage of his wife's method of calculating the tip?

_____

WHAT DO YOU THINK?

A. Discuss the questions in a group.

1. What was your experience of mathematics in school? Was it positive or negative? Explain.

2. Do people leave tips in restaurants in your country? How much do they tip? What other services do people give tips for?

B. Think about Reading 1 and Reading 2 as you discuss the questions. Then choose one question and write five to eight sentences in response.

1. What kinds of things that involve math do you think every adult should know how to do? For example, figuring out the correct tip in a restaurant.

2. Some people have a natural ability in math, while other people struggle with it. Why do you think some people are better at math than others?

Vocabulary Skill	Numbers and mathematical terms	

You will find **numbers** and **mathematical terms** in many texts. You will also use these words in everyday life, such as when you give someone a phone number or when you figure out what to give for a tip. It's important know how to say and write numbers and mathematical terms correctly.

Numbers	
1,000	one thousand
25,000	twenty-five thousand
500,000	five hundred thousand
9,000,000	nine million
802-382-8502	eight oh two, three eight two, eight five oh two
1908	nineteen oh eight

Mathematical terms	
50 + 50 = 100	Fifty plus fifty equals one hundred. OR The sum of fifty and fifty is one hundred.
17 − 5 = 12	Seventeen minus five is twelve. OR Five subtracted from seventeen is twelve.
5 × 5 = 25	Five times five is twenty-five.
81 ÷ 9 = 9	Eighty-one divided by nine equals nine.
$\sqrt{16} = 4$	The square root of sixteen is four.

Note: In math, *is* means the same as *equals*.

Tip for Success

When giving a phone number, people usually say *oh* instead of *zero*.

A. Write out these math problems in words. Then take turns saying them aloud with a partner.

1. $49 \div 7 = 7$ _____

2. $20 \times 4 = 80$ _____

3. $30 \div 6 = 5$ _____

4. $130 + 30 = 160$ _____

5. $30 - 14 = 16$ _____

B. Take turns asking and answering these questions with a partner.

1. How old are your parents?

2. In what year will you be 75 years old?

3. What is the telephone number that you dial most often?

4. In your ideal job, how much money would you like to earn each year?

5. What's the population of your country?

6. In what year did you move into your current house or apartment?

7. How many cousins do you have?

8. What's the address of your favorite place?

Numbers can have more important meanings in our lives.

WRITING

When you write a paragraph, you can use facts to support your ideas. Using **numbers** and **facts** can make your ideas even stronger and more interesting. You can use sources such as books, magazines, and online articles to find numerical facts that support your ideas.

This year, the winter was much colder than usual. This winter's average temperature was **five degrees** below the usual average.

Many people support the president. Currently, **65 percent of the people** think he is doing a good job.

Investments in the stock market have increased. People invested **more than $5 billion** last year.

A. Read the paragraph. Then answer the questions.

> The population of the world is increasing at a dangerous rate. In 1810, the world's population was about one billion people. That figure doubled by 1930. The population reached three billion by 1965, four billion by 1975, and five billion by 1990. By the year 2000, the earth's population was more than six billion people. If the population continues to grow at this rate, the earth may run out of food and water for all of the people who live here.

1. What is the main idea of the paragraph?

   _____

2. What happened in 1930?

   _____

3. What kinds of numbers and facts does the writer use to support his ideas?

   _____

   _____

4. What numbers or information might be helpful to support the idea in the last sentence of the paragraph?

   _____

   _____

B. Read each statement and the numbers in parentheses. Then write a sentence using the numbers to support the idea in the sentence.

1. The cheetah is the fastest animal in the world. It can run very fast. (60 miles per hour)

   The cheetah is the fastest animal in the world. It can run 60 miles per hour.

2. *Titanic* was a very successful movie. It made a lot of money. ($600,788,188 in the U.S. and $1,248,025,607 internationally)

   _____

3. Soccer is a very popular sport. There are many people who play it worldwide. (over 30 million people)

   _____

4. In 2005, many more Americans drove to work instead of using public transportation. (77 percent)

   _____

5. The price of bus tickets in my city is increasing more and more each year. (two years ago, $2.50; price last year, $3.50; price this year, $6.00)

   _____

Grammar   The present perfect

The **present perfect** connects an action in the past with the present. Use it for actions that began in the past and continue up to the present time.

> Alicia **has had** the same English teacher for two years.
> John**'s lived** in New York since 2009.

Sentences that express continuing time up to now often use *for* and *since*.

> I **have known** Luis **for** a long time.
> I**'ve known** him **since** 2007.

The present perfect can also be used for actions that happened at an indefinite (not specific) time in the past.

> Joe **has taken** many math courses.
> I**'ve been** to Brazil, but I **haven't been** to Chile.

> The present perfect is sometimes used for actions that happened repeatedly in the past.
>
> Susana**'s been** to Brazil several times.
>
> Martin**'s taken** algebra **four times.**

A. Complete the paragraph with the present perfect of the verb in parentheses.

Melanie Woods

Melanie Woods _____ math since the mid 1990s. She
          1. (study)
was born in Indiana, but she _____ in California since 2009.
          2. (live)
She is a professor at Stanford University. When Melanie was 16, she was
the first female American to make the U.S. International Math Olympiad
Team. She received silver medals in 1998 and 1999 at the International
Math Olympiad. People _____ in the International Math
          3. (compete)
Olympiad since 1959. Melanie _____ many awards in
          4. (win)
mathematics. She was the first American to be named a Putnam Fellow.
Putnam Fellows receive scholarships for universities. The organization
_____ scholarships to students for over 80 years. In
   5. (provide)
2004, Melanie won the Morgan Prize for her work in mathematics. The
foundation _____ awards to students since 1995. Over the
      6. (give)
years, Melanie Woods _____ a good role model for many
        7. (be)
female mathematicians.

B. Answer these questions using the present perfect. Then compare your answers with a partner.

1. How long have you studied English?

   _____

2. How long have you lived in this city?

   _____

3. How many foreign countries have you visited?

_____

4. How many times have you seen your favorite movie?

_____

5. How long have you known your best friend?

_____

| Unit Assignment | Write a paragraph using numbers to support ideas |

 In this assignment you will write a paragraph about your personal experience of learning math and use numbers to support your ideas. As you prepare your paragraph, think about the Unit Question, "Does everyone need math?" and refer to the Self-Assessment checklist on page 182.

For alternative unit assignments, see the *Q: Skills for Success Teacher's Handbook*.

PLAN AND WRITE

A. BRAINSTORM Think about your experience learning math. Write your positive and negative experiences learning math in the T-chart below.

Positive experiences	Negative experiences

B. PLAN Discuss the notes in your T-chart with a partner. Are there more positive or negative experiences in your chart? Complete the activities.

1. Circle the best ideas from your T-chart.

2. Organize your ideas in the correct order in your notebook. Think about how you can use numbers to support your ideas.

C. **WRITE** Write a topic sentence below that tells if your experience learning math was positive or negative. Then write a paragraph in your notebook. Use numbers and examples to support your ideas. Look at the Self-Assessment checklist below to guide your writing.

Topic sentence: _____

_____

REVISE AND EDIT

 **Critical Thinking**

The Peer Review asks you to **critique** your partner's paragraph. This means you give feedback on what is positive and what is negative. **Critiquing** your partner's writing can help you become better at editing your own work.

A. **PEER REVIEW** Read a partner's paragraph. Answer these questions and discuss them with your partner.

1. Does the paragraph have a clear topic sentence? A clear concluding sentence?

2. Does the paragraph clearly state the ideas?

3. Put a star (★) next to numbers or examples that support ideas. Are the numbers stated clearly to support the idea?

4. Is there anything that is not clear? Put a question mark (?) in the margin next to it.

B. **REWRITE** Review the answers to the questions in Activity A. You may want to revise and rewrite your paragraph.

 **Your Writing Process**

For this activity you could also use Stage 2C, *Editing Checklist* in *Q Online Practice*.

C. **EDIT** Complete the Self-Assessment checklist as you prepare to write the final draft of your paragraph. Be prepared to hand in your work or discuss it in class.

SELF-ASSESSMENT		
Yes	**No**	
☐	☐	Is the first line of the paragraph indented?
☐	☐	Does each sentence start with a capital letter and end with a period or question mark?
☐	☐	Do the subjects and verbs agree?
☐	☐	Is each word spelled correctly? Check a dictionary if you are not sure.
☐	☐	Do you spell or write numbers correctly?
☐	☐	Is there vocabulary from the unit in the paragraph?
☐	☐	Do you use the present perfect? Is it used correctly?

Circle the words you learned in this unit.

Noun
amusement
concept 🔑 AWL
method 🔑 AWL
process 🔑 AWL
recommendation 🔑

Verb
assume 🔑 AWL
determine 🔑
extend 🔑
skip

indicate 🔑 AWL
overestimate AWL
struggle 🔑

Adjective
complicated 🔑
flattered
precise 🔑 AWL
remote 🔑

Phrasal Verb
pick up 🔑
make sense

Phrases
as opposed to

🔑 Oxford 3000™ words
AWL Academic Word List

Check (✓) the skills you learned. If you need more work on a skill, refer to the pages in parentheses.

READING	○	I can make inferences. (p. 169)
VOCABULARY	○	I can use numbers and mathematical terms. (p. 176)
WRITING	○	I can use numbers to support ideas. (p. 178)
GRAMMAR	○	I can use the present perfect. (p. 179)
LEARNING OUTCOME	●	I can describe my personal experience of learning math in a paragraph that includes numbers and facts.

UNIT **10**

Global Health

READING ● synthesizing information
VOCABULARY ● collocations
WRITING ● writing a defining paragraph
GRAMMAR ● adverbs of manner and degree

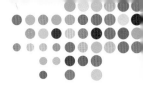

LEARNING OUTCOME

Create a FAQ (Frequently Asked Questions) page about an illness that includes a definition of your topic.

Unit QUESTION

How can we prevent diseases?

PREVIEW THE UNIT

A Discuss these questions with your classmates.

When was the last time you were sick? How did you feel? How did you get sick?

What are some things you do to avoid getting sick?

Look at the photo. Why are the men wearing masks?

B Discuss the Unit Question above with your classmates.

Listen to *The Q Classroom*, **Track 14 on CD 2**, to hear other answers.

185

C Work with a partner. Match the name of each illness with the correct photo.

diabetes	malaria	influenza (flu)
asthma	skin cancer	tuberculosis (TB)

a. _____

b. _____

c. _____

d. _____

e. _____

f. _____

D Write the illness from Activity C next to the correct description.

1. _____: Sun exposure is the leading cause of this disease. This disease causes cells to grow quickly.

2. _____: This is a serious disease that you can get from mosquito bites.

3. _____: This disease affects the lungs and spreads from person to person very easily.

4. _____: This condition causes difficulty in breathing. Using an inhaler (something to help people breathe more easily) can help.

5. _____: With this disease, the body cannot process sugar correctly.

6. _____: With this common illness, a person is sick for one to two weeks.

E Discuss illnesses that spread from person to person with a partner.

READING

READING 1 | Flu FAQ

VOCABULARY

Here are some words from Reading 1. Read the sentences. Then write each word next to the correct definition.

1. Yesterday **approximately** 50 students were home with the flu. I don't know the exact number.

2. You should **cover** your baby with extra blankets in the winter, so he doesn't get cold.

3. I hope my cold doesn't **develop** into a bad cough. It's already worse than it was yesterday.

4. During the **epidemic**, every home in the town had at least one sick family member.

5. Colds are **extremely** common among school children in winter. Both of my children have colds right now.

6. If you have a cold and you sneeze on other people, you can **infect** them.

7. Your overall health is directly **related to** how well you eat and how often you exercise.

8. Pria had a **severe** pain in her back, so I took her to the hospital.

9. A sore throat is a common **symptom** of a cold.

10. A **virus** causes the common cold. It spreads from person to person quickly.

a. _____ (*adj.*) connected with something

b. _____ (*n.*) something that shows that you have an illness

c. _____ (*n.*) a living thing that is too small to see but that makes you sick

d. _____ (*v.*) to put something on or in front of something else to protect it

e. _____ (*v.*) to give a disease to someone

f. _____ (*adj.*) very bad

g. _____ (*adv.*) very

h. _____ (v.) grow slowly, increase, or change into something else

i. _____ (adv.) about; not exactly

j. _____ (n.) a disease that many people in a place have at the same time

PREVIEW READING 1

This is an online FAQ (Frequently Asked Questions) page from a health website about the flu. FAQ sheets state commonly asked questions about a topic, followed by the answers. What symptoms of the flu do you already know?

CD 2
Track 15 **Read the Web page.**

Flu FAQ (Frequently Asked Questions)

Flu season is coming! Are you prepared? Here are answers to your questions!

What is the flu?

1 The flu, short for influenza, is a **virus** that passes easily from person to person. Every year, millions of people miss work and school because of the seasonal flu. Seasonal flu exists worldwide. Usually the flu season is in the winter months, but in warm climates, the flu occurs during the rainy season.

What are the symptoms of the flu?

2 The symptoms of the flu include fever, cough, sore throat, body aches, headache, chills, and fatigue[1]. These **symptoms** usually show up quickly, **developing** within three to six hours of exposure to the virus. With the flu, you may start the day feeling fine, only to end up feeling terrible a few hours later.

What's the difference between the flu and a cold?

3 Both are respiratory[2] illnesses, but they are caused by different viruses. Although the symptoms can be similar, flu symptoms are more **severe** and include a high fever and body aches. Cold symptoms include a runny or stuffy[3] nose and a cough. You may have a slight fever with a cold, but in general, cold symptoms are milder and only last about seven days. The flu can last up to two weeks. It is much more likely to develop into a serious illness and require hospitalization.

Who gets the flu?

4 The seasonal flu is very common all over the world. In the United States, five to 20 percent of the population gets the flu every year. After you have had the flu, you have immunity[4] to that virus. You will not get that

---

[1] **fatigue:** great tiredness
[2] **respiratory:** related to breathing

[3] **stuffy:** blocked, making it hard to breathe
[4] **immunity:** the ability to not get a disease

particular virus again. However, new flu viruses appear every year. Even if you have the flu this year, you will not have immunity to next year's virus. Some people get the flu every year.

Why is the flu dangerous?

5   The flu is especially dangerous for children age two and under, adults over 65 years old, and people in poor health. These people may not be able to fight the virus and can become **extremely** sick. Every year in the U.S., there are **approximately** 36,000 deaths **related to** the seasonal flu.

How does the flu spread?

6   Coughing or sneezing spreads flu viruses from person to person. A virus can live in a tiny drop of liquid from a cough for several hours, and it can live on a surface such as a table for up to 24 hours. A person can **infect** others before flu symptoms even develop and up to five days after becoming sick. You can pass the flu to someone else before you know you are sick.

What's a flu epidemic?

7   A flu **epidemic** is when many people have the flu at the same time, and the number of infected people increases rapidly. Worldwide, annual flu epidemics result in about three to five million cases of severe illness, and about 250,000 to 500,000 deaths.

How can I avoid getting the flu?

8   Many people get a flu vaccine[5] before the flu season starts. The U.S. Center for Disease Control and Prevention says that flu vaccines can prevent 70 percent to 90 percent of infections in healthy people under age 65. However, each year there are new, unknown viruses. Therefore, scientists must develop new vaccines each year. It can take six months to a year to do this. For some viruses, there is no vaccine.

What else can I do?

9   There are many things you can do to stay healthy and prevent the spread of the flu.

- Wash your hands often with soap and water or a liquid hand cleaner. Hand washing is the best way to prevent the spread of flu viruses.
- **Cover** your nose and mouth with a tissue when you cough or sneeze. Throw the tissue in the trash after you use it. If you don't have a tissue, cover your mouth with your arm or shirtsleeve instead of your hands.
- Avoid touching your eyes, nose, or mouth. Viruses can spread this way.
- Avoid sick people.

[5] **vaccine:** a medicine given to people to protect them from a particular disease

MAIN IDEAS

Circle the answer to each question.

1.   What is the purpose of this Web page?
    a.   To provide detailed information about flu deaths around the world.
    b.   To tell readers how to stay healthy and why they should get a vaccine.
    c.   To provide basic information about the flu and how to prevent it.
    d.   To scare readers so that they get the flu vaccine every year.

2. Why is it important to avoid people who are sick with the flu?
   a. They could infect you with the flu.
   b. They should stay in bed.
   c. You may spread a cold to them and make them sicker.
   d. They might not have washed their hands.

3. Based on the information from the FAQ sheet, which of the following can you infer?
   a. Governments give free flu vaccines.
   b. People don't know what the flu is.
   c. The flu is the most difficult global health problem today.
   d. Understanding the flu is important for people around the world.

DETAILS

A. Compare a cold and the flu using the Venn diagram below. Write facts about a cold inside the circle on the right. Write facts about the flu inside the circle on the left. Write facts that are true about both a cold and the flu in the middle.

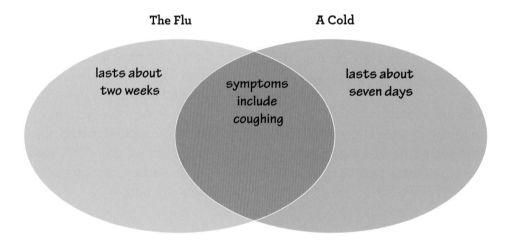

The Flu — lasts about two weeks

symptoms include coughing

A Cold — lasts about seven days

B. Find the answers to these questions in Reading 1.

1. What percentage of people in the United States gets the flu every year?

   _____

2. Why is the flu especially dangerous for elderly people?

   _____

3. After you are infected with the flu, how long will it be before you have symptoms?

   _____

4. How many deaths are related to the flu worldwide each year?

_____

5. What percentage of healthy people under 65 can flu vaccines help in the U.S. every year?

_____

6. How can you prevent the flu from spreading?

_____

 WHAT DO YOU THINK?

Discuss the questions in a group. Then choose one question and write five to eight sentences in response.

1. The reading gives tips on how to avoid getting a cold or the flu. What are some other things you can do?

2. Some people worry a lot about catching the flu from others, and some people are not very concerned. How concerned are you, on a scale from 1 to 10 (10 = extremely concerned, 1 = not concerned at all)? Explain your answers.

3. What other illnesses or diseases are you interested in learning more about? What are they? What do you want to know about them?

Reading Skill | **Synthesizing information**

When you **synthesize** information, you develop a new understanding about a topic by using information from more than one source. For example, you can synthesize information from two different readings to answer a question. You can also synthesize what you already know about a topic and the new information you are learning about that topic from an article you are reading.

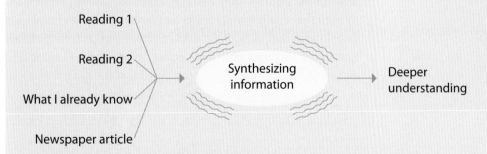

Synthesizing information helps you deepen and expand your knowledge. It is also important because some test questions and writing assignments ask you to synthesize information you have read.

A. Answer these questions.

1. Think back to Reading 1. What information in the reading was new to you? What information did you already know?

_____

_____

2. Read these questions about Reading 1. Which one is a **synthesis** question? Which is a **main idea** question? Which is a **detail** question? Label each one.

a. _____ How does the flu spread?

b. _____ After reading this Web page, will you change any of your health habits? Why or why not?

c. _____ How many people worldwide have a severe case of the flu every year?

3. Answer the questions in item 2. For the synthesis question, be sure to use information that you already know and information from the reading.

a. _____

b. _____

c. _____

B. Read this paragraph. Then answer the synthesis questions, using what you already know, information in the paragraph, and the information in Reading 1.

Just like humans, animals get flu viruses, too. These animal viruses rarely spread to humans, but occasionally they do. For example, an avian flu, also called bird flu, can spread from birds to humans, and H1N1, also called swine flu, can spread from pigs to humans. Once a person gets a virus from an animal, it then spreads very quickly from person to person, just like other types of the flu. Flu viruses that come from animals can be dangerous to humans and can make people extremely sick. People do not have immunity to these new viruses, and it can take a very long time for vaccines to be made. There is often an increased possibility of death with illnesses like the swine flu and avian flu.

1. Is the avian flu more dangerous than the seasonal flu? Explain your answer.

_____

_____

2. How do you think that avian or swine flu can spread from an animal to a human? How does it spread to many people?

_____

_____

READING 2 | More Than a Game

VOCABULARY

A. Here are some words from Reading 2. Read their definitions. Then complete each sentence.

---

area (*n.*) a space used for a particular activity

confusion (*n.*) a state of disorder

damage (*n.*) harm or injury

explore (*v.*) to travel around a place in order to learn about it

global (*adj.*) affecting the whole world

ignore (*v.*) to pay no attention to someone or something

outbreak (*n.*) the sudden appearance of something bad, such as a disease

react to (*phrasal verb*) to do or say something because of something that has happened or is said

reset (*v.*) to change a machine so it gives a different time or number and is ready to use again

virtual (*adj.*) made to appear to exist by computer software or the Internet

---

1. Because the students didn't receive their new schedules, there was

   _____ on the first day of class.

2. Health is not just a local issue. It is a _____ issue that

   requires international cooperation.

3. No one was hurt in the accident, but there was a lot of _____

   to my car.

4. With today's technology, you don't have to leave your home to see interesting

   wild animals. You can just go online and visit a _____ zoo.

5. When the power came back on, we had to _____ all of the

   clocks in the house.

6. In the local elementary school, there was a(an) _____ of the chicken pox. Many children got the illness at the same time.

7. Traveling to new countries is very exciting. I love to _____ new places.

8. There is one _____ in the museum where you can use your cell phone. You can't talk on your cell in any other places.

9. Police officers and firefighters are trained to _____ dangerous situations quickly.

10. You shouldn't _____ flu symptoms and hope they will go away. You should go see a doctor.

PREVIEW READING 2

This is a magazine article about a popular virtual game called World of Warcraft. It is played online with thousands of players. This game has a complicated virtual world with many characters.

Do you think a virtual game could help you understand how people behave?

☐ Yes   ☐ No

CD 2
Track 16   **Read the magazine article.**

More Than a Game

1   In 2005, a new virus caused a frightening pandemic[1], with hundreds of thousands of deaths around the world. Travelers and pets spread this deadly virus in only a few hours, and it seemed unstoppable. Fortunately, the pandemic took place in a **virtual** world, and those who died were avatars[2], not real people. The pandemic? A blood virus. The place? *World of Warcraft*, an online computer game with more than 6.5 million players at the time of the **outbreak**.

2   *World of Warcraft* is one of the most popular online games in the world. Players move their characters, known as avatars, around the game's imaginary world. The avatars **explore** new places,

---

[1] **pandemic:** outbreak of a disease that occurs in many areas of the world at one time

[2] **avatar:** a picture on a computer screen of a person or an animal, which represents a real person

World of Warcraft

fight scary monsters, search for wealth, and interact with other players. In 2005, the game's maker, Blizzard Entertainment Inc., created a very powerful virus and put it in a few of the game's **areas** as a challenge for the most advanced players. The company tried to keep the virus in only certain areas, but just as would happen in real life, the virus escaped. Disaster followed.

3   Nina Fefferman and Eric Lofgren are scientists who studied the game virus. They reported that the game virus was very much like a real disease. Within hours of its release, *World of Warcraft* was in a state of **confusion**. The disease had quickly spread to the game's most populated cities.

4   In the real world, people can travel great distances quickly and easily by air. The avatars in *World of Warcraft* could do the same. Since the virus was extremely strong, it rapidly spread to all areas of the virtual world. Sick and infected avatars did not quarantine[3] themselves, so they infected others everywhere they went. The virus also spread to the avatars' pets. Soon dead avatars were everywhere in *World of Warcraft*. Blizzard Entertainment tried to stop the virus and told players to stay offline and not play the game until the pandemic was over. But players were very curious, so they went into infected areas to see the **damage**. When they did this, they became infected and died. Because players **ignored** the quarantine, the virus spread extremely fast. Finally, Blizzard had to **reset** the entire game and bring the dead avatars back to life.

5   Fefferman and Lofgren believe that it is important to study how people react in a simulation[4] of a pandemic. Scientific knowledge about viruses and developing vaccines is very important for preventing disease. Experts say that knowing how to slow the spread of a pandemic is also essential for **global** health. Online simulations of pandemics allow scientists to study how people behave and make decisions, and how their behavior affects the spread of a deadly virus. Fefferman and Lofgren are working with Blizzard to use viruses in other games so that researchers can learn more about human behavior in a pandemic. Understanding how humans might **react to** a health emergency will help experts control the spread of a virus.

---

[3] **quarantine:** to take a person who has a disease and separate them from others

[4] **simulation:** a game or event that creates the effect or appearance of a real situation

MAIN IDEAS

Answer these questions.

1. Where did the virus take place?

_____

2. How did the outbreak start in World of Warcraft?

   _____

3. What happened to the characters that became infected?

   _____

4. How did Blizzard Entertainment finally stop the outbreak?

   _____

5. Why did Fefferman and Lofgren study the game?

   _____

DETAILS

Complete the flow chart with details from the reading.

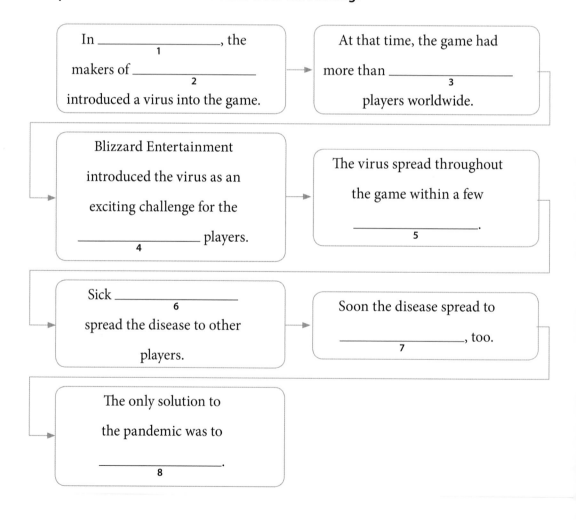

In _____, the makers of _____ introduced a virus into the game.

1

2

→

At that time, the game had more than _____ players worldwide.

3

Blizzard Entertainment introduced the virus as an exciting challenge for the _____ players.

4

→

The virus spread throughout the game within a few _____.

5

Sick _____ spread the disease to other players.

6

→

Soon the disease spread to _____, too.

7

The only solution to the pandemic was to _____.

8

 **WHAT DO YOU THINK?**

A. Discuss the questions in a group.

1. In *World of Warcraft*, some players entered dangerous, infected areas because they were curious. Do you think that this might happen in a real pandemic? Explain.

Tip Critical Thinking
Question 2 of Activity B asks you to **recommend** or suggest ways to prevent a problem (the flu). **Recommending** means that you are deciding what is a good thing to do. This can help you better understand a problem and its possible solutions.

2. Do you think that experts can learn useful information about human behavior by studying how people behave when they play simulation games? Why or why not?

B. Think about both Reading 1 and Reading 2 as you discuss the questions. Then choose one question and write five to eight sentences in response.

1. Imagine that an epidemic spreads quickly and becomes a global pandemic. What kinds of problems do you think there might be for government and doctors?

2. The flu can spread rapidly in schools and cause teachers and children to become sick. What can a school do to prevent the spread of the flu?

Vocabulary Skill | Collocations

A **collocation** is a group of words that frequently go together. Some collocations are made up of a verb + a preposition. Here are some common verb + preposition collocations with the prepositions *on*, *to*, and *in*.

comment on (to give an opinion about)

contribute to (to give a part to the total of something)

increase in (to become or make something larger)

participate in (to share or join in)

succeed in (to manage to achieve what you want, do well)

in response to (an answer or reaction to something)

in favor of (to support somebody or something, to prefer)

in common (like or similar to somebody or something)

Using collocations will help your speaking and writing sound more natural.

A. Complete each sentence below with the correct collocation.

comment on	contribute to	increase in	in favor of
participate in	succeed in	in response to	in common

1. A cold and the flu have some things _____. For example, they can both be passed from one person to another.

2. My mother told me she liked my new dress, but she didn't _____ my new haircut. Maybe she doesn't like it.

3. The scientists need 50 people to _____ a study for a new flu vaccine. They will pay each person $500.

4. There's been a(n) _____ cases of the flu this winter. It's much worse than last year.

5. Eating lots of green vegetables can _____ your overall health.

6. Sofia nodded her head _____ my question.

7. If you want to _____ becoming an Olympic athlete, you have to train very hard.

8. Keiko was not _____ of the new proposal, so she voted against it.

B. Choose five of the collocations from Activity A. Write a sentence using each one.

_____

_____

_____

_____

_____

WRITING

Writing Skill   Writing a defining paragraph

A **defining paragraph** defines and explains a term or concept. Use a defining paragraph when you want to explain a term or concept that your reader might not know.

Use these guidelines to make your defining paragraph clear to your reader.

- First, write a topic sentence that states the term or concept and defines it.
- Make sure the definition is clear. Use a dictionary or online sources to help you.
- Then write about the term or concept using explanations and examples. Examples help a reader understand your ideas.
- You may want to explain how the term or concept is different from similar terms.
- You may want to help your reader understand the term or concept by explaining what it is not.

You can use these sentence structures to write a topic sentence for a defining paragraph.

_____ is a _____ that _____.

An <u>inhaler</u> is a <u>device</u> that <u>helps a person with asthma breathe</u>.

_____ is when _____.

An <u>epidemic</u> is when <u>many people have an illness at the same time</u>.

A. Read this defining paragraph. Then answer the questions.

A pandemic is an epidemic that has spread to several countries or continents, becoming a global health emergency. An epidemic can develop into a pandemic very quickly. For example, in 2003, the SARS (Severe Acute Respiratory Syndrome) virus spread from China to 37 countries around the world in just a few weeks. The avian flu and the swine flu have both caused pandemics in recent years. In 2009, a new type of flu virus started in Mexico in April and spread to 70 countries in eight weeks. A month later, the number of countries nearly doubled. A pandemic is not the same as a plague, which is a disease that spreads quickly and kills many people. A pandemic can also kill many people, but it doesn't always. However, a pandemic is a very serious international health emergency.

1. What is the definition of pandemic?

_____

2. What term is pandemic similar to?

_____

3. What examples of pandemics does the writer give?

_____

4. What does the writer say a pandemic is not?

_____

B. Write a topic sentence for a defining paragraph for each of these topics. Use your own words.

1. A common cold

_____

2. The flu

_____

3. Asthma

_____

4. An online simulation game

_____

C. Choose one of the topics in Activity B and write a defining paragraph in your notebook.

| Grammar | Adverbs of manner and degree | |

An **adverb of manner** describes how something is done or how something happens. It usually comes after the verb or object.

Our team played **hard** and won the game **easily**.
verb   adverb   verb   object   adverb

In sentences with an auxiliary verb, *-ly* adverbs of manner can come between the auxiliary verb and the main verb.

His temperature was **rapidly** rising during the afternoon.
auxiliary   adverb   verb

An **adverb of degree** tells to what degree something is done or happens. It comes before an adjective or before another adverb.

It was an **especially** difficult exam.
<u>adverb</u> <u>adjective</u>

The man was breathing **fairly** slowly.
<u>adverb</u> adverb

Here are some common adverbs of degree:

greater degree   **lesser degree**

← extremely   especially   very   really   so   fairly   quite   pretty   somewhat   hardly →

A. Write the adverb form of each of the adjectives below. Then complete the sentences with the correct adverb of manner.

common _____	slow _____
success _____	bright _____
frequent _____	serious _____
precise _____	rapid ____rapidly____

1. The temperature in New York can change very _____rapidly_____. One day it's warm. The next day it's cold.

2. Doctors have not been able to _____ cure the common cold.

3. The sun shines _____ through my window every morning and wakes me up.

4. Sonia followed the instructions _____, because she didn't want to make a mistake.

5. Mercedes talks to her family _____. She calls them three or four times a week.

6. I need to think about the situation very _____ before I make a decision.

7. Please drive _____. There are a lot of young children in this neighborhood.

8. Orange trees are not _____ found in cold places.

B. Complete the sentences with your own ideas and opinions. Then read your sentences to a partner.

Tip for Success

Don't overuse the adverbs *very* and *really*. They are useful general terms, but more specific adverbs give more information and make your writing more interesting.

1. I think _____ is really interesting.

2. In my opinion _____ is extremely _____.

3. I can _____ fairly well.

4. For me _____ is extremely difficult.

5. I have had a(n) _____ _____ day today.

Unit Assignment | **Write an FAQ Page**

 In this assignment, you are going to write a FAQ page about an illness. You will include a definition of the topic in your FAQ page and information on how the illness can be prevented. As you prepare your FAQ page, think about the Unit Question, "How can we prevent diseases?" and refer to the Self-Assessment checklist on page 204.

For alternative unit assignments, see the *Q: Skills for Success Teacher's Handbook*.

PLAN AND WRITE

A. BRAINSTORM Complete the activities.

1. Brainstorm a list for each question in your notebook. Write down as many ideas as you can.
   - What illnesses do you know of that can spread from person to person?
   - What are some illnesses that you or someone you know have had?
   - What illnesses have you learned about recently?

2. Discuss your ideas with a partner. Choose one idea to write about.

3. Choose the illness you are going to write about.

B. PLAN Organize the information about your topic. Remember, your goal is to provide useful information to your readers.

1. Fill in these FAQs with the illness you chose. Then write notes to answer each question.

   a. What is _____?

   _____

   _____

b. What are the symptoms of _____?

_____

_____

c. How is _____ different from other diseases?

_____

_____

d. Who gets _____?

_____

_____

e. How does _____ spread?

_____

_____

f. How can you avoid getting _____?

_____

_____

g. How can we prevent the spread of _____?

_____

_____

2. Look at your notes. Are there any questions you will not include? Are there any additional questions that you want to include? Make any changes needed.

3. What additional information do you need? Where can you get that information? Find the information you need and add it to your notes.

C. **WRITE** Write your FAQ page in your notebook, using your notes in Activity B. Start with a defining paragraph that clearly explains your illness. Then continue with other questions and answers. Try to use some adverbs of manner and degree. Look at the Self-Assessment checklist on page 204 to guide your writing.

REVISE AND EDIT

A. **PEER REVIEW** Read your partner's FAQ page. Answer these questions and discuss them with your partner.

1. Is there a defining paragraph at the beginning? Is it clear?

2. Is each question answered? In other words, does the answer relate directly to the question?

3. Is there an answer that is not clear? Put a question mark (?) in the margin next to it.

4. What is the most interesting question or information?

5. Did you learn anything new? Explain.

B. **REWRITE** Review the answers to the questions in Activity A. You may want to revise and rewrite your FAQ page.

C. **EDIT** Complete the Self-Assessment checklist as you prepare to write the final draft of your FAQ page. Be prepared to hand in your work or discuss it in class.

Your Writing Process

For this activity you could also use Stage 2C, *Personal Editing Checklist* in *Q Online Practice*.

Yes	No	SELF-ASSESSMENT
☐	☐	Does each sentence start with a capital letter and end with a period or question mark?
☐	☐	Do the subjects and verbs agree?
☐	☐	Is each word spelled correctly? Check a dictionary if you are not sure.
☐	☐	Is there vocabulary from the unit in the FAQ page?
☐	☐	Do you have adverbs of manner in your FAQ page? Do you use the correct word order?
☐	☐	Do you have adverbs of degree in your FAQ page? Do you use the correct word order? Do you have a good variety of adverbs?

Track Your Success

Circle the words you learned in this unit.

Nouns
area 🔑 AWL
confusion 🔑
damage 🔑
epidemic
outbreak
symptom
virus 🔑

Verbs
cover 🔑
develop 🔑
explore 🔑
ignore 🔑 AWL

infect
react to 🔑 AWL
reset

Adjectives
global 🔑 AWL
related to 🔑
severe 🔑
virtual AWL

Adverbs
approximately 🔑 AWL
extremely 🔑

Collocations
comment on
contribute to
in common
increase in
in favor of
in response to
participate in
succeed in

🔑 Oxford 3000™ words
AWL Academic Word List

Check (✓) the skills you learned. If you need more work on a skill, refer to the page(s) in parentheses.

READING ●	I can synthesize information. (p. 191)
VOCABULARY ●	I can use collocations. (p. 197)
WRITING ●	I can write a defining paragraph. (p. 199)
GRAMMAR ●	I can use adverbs of manner and degree. (pp. 200–201)
LEARNING OUTCOME ●	I can create a FAQ (Frequently Asked Questions) page about an illness that includes a definition of my topic.